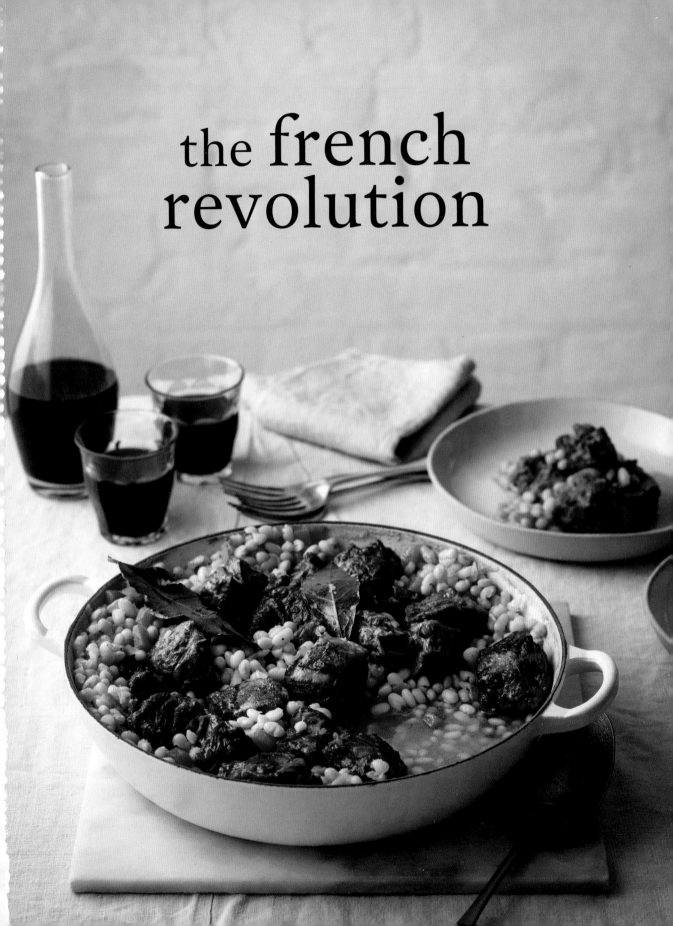

the french revolution

MICHEL ROUX JR

the french revolution

140 Classic Recipes made Fresh & Simple

SEVEN DIALS

CONTENTS

INTRODUCTION

The food in this book is a celebration of the great French way of life and way of eating, but with a difference. French cuisine has a reputation for being rich, complex and time-consuming, which it can be, particularly in restaurants. But French home cooking is based on good, local, seasonal ingredients and simple skills. This is the food I was brought up on and that I still like to eat – the food we enjoy cooking as a family. It's fresh and delicious, with vegetables, pulses and fruit playing a large part.

In France, as in Britain, people are keen to have a healthier diet and I believe we can achieve this without compromising on taste or pleasure. In this book I've created some brand new recipes to suit the way we like to eat today, as well as taking a fresh look at some much-loved traditional dishes to bring them up to date. These days, most of us don't have hours to spend cooking – and then washing every pot and pan in the place – so I've included plenty of recipes that take very little time but are still full of flavour. There are speedy omelettes, snacks such as open sandwiches and dips, bean and lentil recipes and plenty of pasta. I was raised on pasta and it's still one of my top choices for a quick supper. There's a wide selection of fish and meat too, ranging from simple and cheap mackerel fillets to more elaborate weekend feasts, such as shrimp tartlets thermidor and rack of lamb.

The food here is very achievable – you don't need lots of fancy equipment and nearly all of the ingredients are easy to come by. Wherever possible I have reduced the richness and used less cream and butter than in the old days, while maintaining flavour. But this is not a diet book and there are some classics that just can't be improved on. I believe it's fine to have a more indulgent treat once in a while so you will find a few luxurious dishes, such as duck confit pie and French toast.

In the following chapters you will find ideas for all times of day from sensational scrambled eggs to soups, salads, easy one-pot suppers such as Basque-style chicken, mussels with beer, and braised squid, as well as puddings, breads and some special French drinks that make great aperitifs. There are recipes from every region to give a glimpse of what different parts of France have to offer. The recipes are not extravagant – there's no lobster or foie gras. I only mention truffles a couple of times – and even then they're optional.

One of the best things about cooking great food is sharing it with other people. I hope you will enjoy making these dishes for your family and friends and showing them just how simple and delicious good French food can be.

COOK'S NOTES

Bayonne ham – this is an air-dried ham that comes from Southwest France and is named after the city of Bayonne. If you can't get Bayonne ham, you can use other air-dried hams, such as Parma ham or Serrano ham.

Bouquet garni – this is a bundle of herbs tied together with string for adding to soups, casseroles and other dishes. Tying the herbs together makes it easier to remove them when the dish is done. The classic version contains parsley stalks, bay leaf, thyme, celery and leek, but I sometimes vary the contents to match the dish.

Butter – I use unsalted butter in recipes, unless otherwise specified. I do think that butter is one of those things that is worth spending a bit extra on if you can, in order to get the best.

Eggs –I use large, free-range eggs unless otherwise specified.

Parsley – I'm happy with either curly or flatleaf parsley for most recipes, unless specified.

Piment d'espelette – this is a mild, smoky chilli pepper grown in the Basque region of France. The chillies are dried and used whole, flaked or ground. You can use ordinary chilli powder or flakes but some kinds may be hotter than the Espelette chilli so bear this in mind.

Stocks – at the back of this book you will find recipes for some basics, such as stocks. Stock is really worth making yourself, but if you don't have time you can buy some good fresh stocks in supermarkets now.

Ventrèche – this comes from fatty pork belly and can be smoked or salted. Pancetta or smoked streaky bacon are good substitutes if you can't get ventrèche.

SUR LE POUCE

Fast Food

The French term 'sur le pouce' means on the go and is generally used to describe fast food. I'm not a fan of the usual sort of fast food, but sometimes we all need to put together something good to eat in a hurry. This chapter includes my idea of fast food – omelettes and other egg dishes, open sandwiches or tartines, and dips. All are quick, easy and delicious.

OEUFS BROUILLÉS AUX ANCHOIS ET OLIVES

Scrambled Eggs with Anchovies

My favourite sort of fast food, this dish is popular all along the French Mediterranean coast. It's made with simple store-cupboard ingredients but it has bags of flavour and is good served at any time of day. If you don't like the saltiness of anchovies, give them a thorough rinse under cold water.

Serves 4

12 GOOD-QUALITY SALTED ANCHOVIES IN OLIVE OIL

1 TBSP OLIVE OIL

2 GARLIC CLOVES, PEELED AND CHOPPED

10 FREE-RANGE EGGS

1 TBSP COLD BUTTER

24 GREEN OLIVES, PITTED AND HALVED

CHIVES OR SPRING ONION LEAVES, SNIPPED

TOAST, TO SERVE

SALT AND FRESHLY GROUND BLACK PEPPER

Finely chop 4 of the anchovies. Warm the oil in a heavy-based pan, then gently cook the chopped anchovies and garlic. Take the pan off the heat and leave to cool.

Cut the remaining anchovies in half lengthways. Beat the eggs in a bowl, but do not season them.

Pour the eggs into the pan with the chopped anchovies and garlic and cook them over a medium heat, while stirring with a spatula or wooden spoon. When the eggs are cooked but still a little runny, take the pan off the heat and mix in the butter.

Check the seasoning and add salt and pepper if needed. Spoon the eggs into bowls and arrange the halved anchovies and olives on top. Finish with some snipped chives or spring onion leaves, then serve at once with some toast.

CROQUE-MADAME AU FOUR AVEC OEUFS DE CAILLE

Baked Croque-Madame with Quails' Eggs

The traditional croque-madame is made with a rich béchamel sauce and is usually fried. My baked version is just as delicious but less calorific and much easier to make for a crowd, as it is baked in the oven. The bulk of the preparation can be done in advance if you like.

Serves 6

225G STALE BREAD (SOURDOUGH IS BEST)

3 FREE-RANGE EGGS, PLUS 2 YOLKS

600ML MILK

100ML DOUBLE CREAM

1 TSP DIJON MUSTARD

90G GRUYÈRE CHEESE, GRATED

90G COMTÉ CHEESE, GRATED

GENEROUS GRATING OF NUTMEG

2 TBSP BUTTER

200G GOOD-QUALITY COOKED HAM, SLICED

6 QUAILS' EGGS

SALT AND FRESHLY GROUND BLACK PEPPER

Preheat the oven to 220°C/Fan 200°C/Gas 7. Cut the bread into 3cm cubes, put them on a baking tray and toast them in the oven until they're dry and lightly coloured. Remove the bread and leave the oven on.

Whisk the 3 eggs, 2 yolks, milk and cream together in a bowl. Add the mustard and grated cheeses and season with nutmeg, salt and pepper.

Generously butter a roasting tin. Add a layer of bread cubes, then enough of the egg and cheese mixture to cover, followed by some slices of ham. Repeat the layers twice more until all the bread, egg mixture and ham are used up. Leave to stand for 5 minutes, pressing the layers down with a spatula to make sure the bread absorbs the liquid.

Bake in the oven for 20 minutes – you can prepare the dish in advance to this point. Take the tin out and carefully crack the quails' eggs on top, spacing them evenly. Put the tin back in the oven, turn the temperature down to 200°C/Fan 180°C/Gas 6 and bake for another 10–12 minutes or until the quails' eggs are just cooked.

Cut the croque-madame into portions, making sure there is an egg on each serving.

CROQUE-MONSIEUR
Baked Cheese Sandwich

The classic French cheese toastie is made with a béchamel sauce, but this is my quicker, lighter version. It's a good way of using up any scraps of cheese in the fridge – a mixture is good – but it is important to use good-quality bread. As for the ham, cooked or air-dried are both fine and I have even used bresaola and salami.

Serves 4

200G GRATED CHEESE (I LIKE GRUYÈRE, COMTÉ AND SOME GOATS' CHEESE, SUCH AS A CROTTIN)

2 TBSP DIJON MUSTARD

4 TBSP CRÈME FRAÎCHE

1 SMALL RED ONION, FINELY CHOPPED

GRATING OF NUTMEG

8 SLICES OF BREAD

8 SLICES OF GOOD-QUALITY COOKED HAM

FRESHLY GROUND BLACK PEPPER

Mix the grated cheese with the mustard, crème fraîche and onion and season with nutmeg and black pepper. Preheat the oven to 230°C/Fan 210°C/Gas 8.

Lightly toast the bread, then take about a third of the cheese mixture and spread it on to 4 of the slices. Add 2 slices of ham to each one, then some more of the cheese. Top with the remaining slices of bread and spread the rest of the cheese mix over them.

Put the sandwiches on a baking sheet and bake them in the oven for 10 minutes. If the sandwiches are not brown enough, give them a quick blast under a hot grill.

OEUFS AUX ÉPINARDS

Baked Eggs with Spinach

I usually make this simple family favourite with hens' eggs but it is also great with duck eggs, which have a richer and deeper flavour. I like to serve this with some good bread and perhaps a few shavings of hard cheese, such as Cantal.

Serves 2

1 TBSP OLIVE OIL

2 GARLIC CLOVES, PEELED AND FINELY CHOPPED

300G SPINACH, WASHED

2 TBSP CRÈME FRAÎCHE

GRATING OF NUTMEG

4 FREE-RANGE EGGS

SHAVINGS OF CHEESE, SUCH AS CANTAL (OPTIONAL)

SALT AND FRESHLY GROUND BLACK PEPPER

Preheat the oven to 200°C/Fan 180°C/Gas 6. Heat the olive oil in a pan, then add the garlic and cook it gently until soft without allowing it to brown. Add the spinach and let it wilt.

Tip the spinach into a sieve to drain and press it to get rid of as much water as you can. Transfer the spinach to a food processor, add the crème fraîche and blitz until smooth. Season with nutmeg, salt and pepper. Pour this mixture into an ovenproof dish, about 20 x 30cm in size, spreading it to about 2cm thick.

Break the eggs on top. Put the dish in the oven and bake for about 12 minutes or until the whites of the eggs are set. Serve at once, scattered with some shavings of cheese, if using.

OEUF MAYONNAISE
Egg Mayonnaise

I'm more than happy to eat eggs at any time of day. This recipe for egg mayonnaise is lighter than the usual, as I make it with a little cream cheese and oil instead of mayonnaise. Served with a touch of chilli oil and some crispy chicken skin it's a real treat – most butchers will give you some chicken skin if you ask. Good with sourdough toast.

Serves 4

4 FREE-RANGE EGGS (AT ROOM TEMPERATURE)

1 TSP DIJON MUSTARD

1 TBSP VEGETABLE OIL

1 TBSP CREAM CHEESE

4 PIECES OF CHICKEN SKIN, ABOUT THE SIZE OF YOUR HAND

SALT AND FRESHLY GROUND BLACK PEPPER

Chilli Oil

300ML OLIVE OIL

1 TBSP PIMENT D'ESPELETTE (SEE PAGE 8) OR CHILLI FLAKES

2 TSP TOMATO PASTE

Bring a pan of water to the boil, add the eggs and cook them for 7 minutes. Drain, then put them in a bowl of iced water to stop them cooking any more.

Carefully peel the eggs and cut them in half. The yolks should be almost set – not hard. Remove the yolks and put them in a bowl or blender – set the whites aside. Add the mustard, oil and cream cheese to the yolks, then season well with salt and black pepper and mix until smooth.

Preheat the oven to 200°C/Fan 180°C/Gas 6. Scrape the chicken skins and remove any feathers. Place the skins on a roasting tray lined with greaseproof paper and season them with salt and pepper. Bake in the oven for 20–30 minutes until the skin is golden and crisp.

For the chilli oil, put all the ingredients in a blender and blitz until smooth. Pour the oil into a jar. This makes more than you need for this recipe but you can store the oil in the fridge for up to 3 weeks.

To serve, pile the yolk mixture back into the halves. Break up the pieces of chicken skin and scatter them on top, then add a drizzle of chilli oil.

OEUFS COCOTTES ARDÈCHOISE

Baked Eggs with Chestnuts

The Ardèche is the main chestnut-growing region in France, so plenty of the local dishes contain chestnuts. They make a nice addition to this baked egg recipe, which is quick and easy to make and very tasty to eat. You can use vacuum-packed chestnuts if you like.

Serves 4

BUTTER, FOR GREASING

1 TBSP OLIVE OIL

6–8 CEPS (FROZEN ARE FINE), WIPED AND SLICED

2 GARLIC CLOVES, CHOPPED

1 TBSP CHOPPED PARSLEY

4 LARGE COOKED CHESTNUTS, SHELLED AND ROUGHLY CHOPPED

4 FREE-RANGE EGGS

360ML DOUBLE CREAM

SALT AND FRESHLY GROUND BLACK PEPPER

You need 4 ramekins or ovenproof dishes measuring about 5cm high and 8cm in diameter. Lightly butter the insides. Preheat the oven to 200°C/Fan 180°C/Gas 6.

Heat the oil in a frying pan and gently sauté the sliced ceps. Add the garlic and parsley, then season with salt and pepper.

Divide the ceps between the dishes and add the chestnuts. Break an egg into each dish, then divide the cream between them. Season with a little salt and pepper.

Place the dishes in a roasting tin and add enough just-boiled water to come halfway up the sides. Bake in the preheated oven for 12–15 minutes, then serve straightaway.

OEUFS BROUILLÉS AUX ESCARGOTS

Scrambled Eggs with Snails

I remember gathering snails with my father when I was a child and going through the very long process of purging, then cooking them. Now we always have a jar or tin of snails in the cupboard ready to devour. This is a fairly rich and indulgent dish, but now and then it's good to be naughty. I've made the crème fraîche optional but for my father it's essential!

Serves 4

2 TBSP BUTTER

1 SHALLOT, PEELED AND CHOPPED

1 GARLIC CLOVE, PEELED AND CHOPPED

120G COOKED SNAILS, DRAINED

10 FREE-RANGE EGGS, LIGHTLY BEATEN

1 TBSP PASTIS

2 TBSP CRÈME FRAÎCHE (OPTIONAL)

4 TBSP CHOPPED PARSLEY

LEAVES FROM A BUNCH OF WATERCRESS, WASHED

SALT AND FRESHLY GROUND BLACK PEPPER

Melt a tablespoon of the butter in a pan, add the shallot and garlic and cook them gently until softened. Add the drained snails, coat them in the butter and season with salt and pepper. Take the pan off the heat and set aside.

Meanwhile, pour the eggs into a separate pan and cook them slowly over a medium heat, stirring with a spatula or wooden spoon. Once the eggs are cooked but still a little runny, take the pan off the heat and mix in the remaining butter.

Add the pastis and the crème fraiche, if using, to the snails and simmer for 30 seconds, then add the parsley and watercress.

Serve the scrambled eggs topped with the snails.

OMELETTE AUX BLETTES
Swiss Chard Omelette

Swiss chard is full of flavour and goodness. This omelette is delicious for a quick lunch and also nice served cold for a snack or to take on a picnic.

Serves 4

400G BABY SWISS CHARD, WASHED

120G PANCETTA OR VENTRÈCHE (SEE PAGE 8), DICED

1 SHALLOT, PEELED AND CHOPPED

1 GARLIC CLOVE, PEELED AND CHOPPED

1 TBSP OLIVE OIL

1 TBSP BUTTER

6–8 FREE-RANGE EGGS

50G GRUYÈRE OR EMMENTAL CHEESE, GRATED

RED WINE VINEGAR

SALT AND FRESHLY GROUND BLACK PEPPER

Wash the chard well and remove any damaged leaves or stalks. Bring a pan of water to the boil, season it with salt, then add the chard and cook it for 3–4 minutes. Drain and refresh the chard in a bowl of iced water to stop the cooking process. When the chard is cold, drain it again and squeeze out as much moisture as you can. Roughly chop the leaves and stalks.

Add the pancetta or ventrèche to a frying pan over a medium heat and cook until it has rendered some of its fat. Add the shallot, garlic and oil and cook for 2–3 minutes, then add the chard, season well and fry for another couple of minutes. Tip everything into a bowl.

Heat the butter in the same frying pan until foaming. Beat the eggs in a bowl with the cheese, then add the chard mixture. Pour this into the pan and stir with a spatula until it starts to set. Cover the pan with a lid and leave the omelette to cook gently for 6–8 minutes until completely set.

Don't fold this omelette – turn it out on to a plate and cut it into 4 wedges. Sprinkle with a few drops of vinegar and serve at once.

OMELETTE SOUFFLÉE AU FROMAGE
Souffléed Cheese Omelette

This is halfway between an omelette and a soufflé and makes a delicious quick meal. I like to use Comté cheese but any kind will do. Once you've mastered the basic recipe, you can try adding extras such as ham or chopped herbs to the mix. Anything goes! A little side salad is all you need with this.

Serves 2

4 FREE-RANGE EGGS, SEPARATED

2 PINCHES OF SALT

1 TBSP BUTTER

100G HARD CHEESE SUCH AS COMTÉ, GRATED

FRESHLY GROUND BLACK PEPPER

Preheat the oven to 200°C/Fan 180°C/Gas 6.

Whisk the egg whites with the salt until they form firm peaks. Whisk the egg yolks in a separate bowl, then whisk in one-third of the whites. Gently fold in the remaining whites.

Melt the butter in a non-stick, ovenproof frying pan, then pour in the eggs. Leave the pan on the hob for 20 seconds, then sprinkle on the cheese and season with black pepper. Transfer the pan to the preheated oven for 5 minutes, then divide the omelette in half and serve.

TAPENADE

Black Olive Paste

This is one of those French classics that really can't be improved on. Use it as a dip, spread it liberally on toast, or use a spoonful to liven up a salad dressing. Wonderful.

Serves 6–8

6 SALTED ANCHOVY FILLETS

200G PITTED BLACK OLIVES (NIÇOISE ARE BEST)

1 TBSP CAPERS IN BRINE, RINSED

JUICE OF 1 LEMON

1 TSP CHOPPED THYME

1 GARLIC CLOVE, CRUSHED (OPTIONAL)

4 TBSP EXTRA VIRGIN OLIVE OIL

FRESHLY GROUND BLACK PEPPER

Rinse the anchovies in cold water and pat them dry. Place them in a blender with the olives, capers, lemon juice, thyme and garlic, if using, and blitz. Scoop the mixture into a bowl, then stir in the oil and season with black pepper.

Cover the bowl and store in the fridge. Tapenade keeps well for about 2 weeks.

AÏOLI

Garlic Mayonnaise

I always like to have some aïoli in the fridge. Using a whole egg and some vegetable oil makes this less rich than the traditional recipe. Be sure to remove any green bits from the garlic cloves, as they can make the mixture bitter and may be heavy on the digestion.

Makes a big bowlful

4–6 GARLIC CLOVES, PEELED AND ROUGHLY CHOPPED

1 FREE-RANGE EGG

2 TSP DIJON MUSTARD

JUICE OF 1 LEMON

PINCH OF SALT

250ML SUNFLOWER OIL

125ML OLIVE OIL

Put the garlic in a blender with the egg, mustard, lemon juice and salt. Blitz for a few seconds until the mixture starts to emulsify. Then, with the motor running, slowly pour in the oils.

Scoop the aïoli into a bowl and cover. Serve with socca (see page 34), sticks of raw vegetables, whatever you like. This keeps well in the fridge for about a week.

ANCHOÏADE

Anchovy Dip

Serve this classic dip with sticks of raw vegetables or spread it on toast for a tasty snack. My version is lighter than the usual recipe and contains less oil.

Serves 6–8

200G SALTED ANCHOVIES

4 GARLIC CLOVES, PEELED AND CRUSHED

80ML EXTRA VIRGIN OLIVE OIL

2 TBSP WHITE WINE VINEGAR

2 TBSP ROUGHLY CHOPPED PARSLEY

FRESHLY GROUND BLACK PEPPER

Rinse the anchovies under cold water to remove excess salt, then pat them dry.

Place the anchovies in a blender with the garlic and blitz to a smooth paste. With the motor still running, add the oil and vinegar and season with black pepper. Serve garnished with chopped parsley.

SOCCA

Chickpea Pancakes

Street food from Nice, socca are simple, cheap and addictive! Serve them with dips such as tapenade (see page 30) or aïoli (see page 32) and grilled aubergines, or with salads. They're fine finished under a grill, but if you have a wood-fired oven they will be even more delicious.

Makes about 8

150G CHICKPEA (GRAM) FLOUR

1 TSP SALT

½ TSP GROUND CUMIN

OLIVE OIL

FRESHLY GROUND BLACK PEPPER

Mix the flour, salt and cumin in a bowl and season with pepper. Then whisk in 320ml of water and a tablespoon of oil to make a nice smooth batter. It should have a pouring consistency, like thick double cream. Cover the bowl and leave the batter to rest for an hour.

Preheat your grill. Heat an ovenproof frying pan and grease it with a tablespoon of oil. Pour in just enough batter to cover the base of the pan and use the back of a spoon or palette knife to spread it evenly to a thickness of about 5–10mm. Leave the pan on the hob until the batter sets, then place it under the hot grill until the socca blisters and even burns a little around the edges. Tip it out on to a board and repeat until you've used all the batter.

Serve the socca with dips or simply drizzle them with oil and season with salt.

TARTINE BOURGUIGNONNE

Open Sandwich with Beef, Shallots & Watercress

Tartines, or open sandwiches, are a great light meal and a good way to use up leftovers! These are excellent with leftover roast beef, or you could cook a steak specially and slice it.

Serves 4

2 SHALLOTS, PEELED AND SLICED

200ML RED WINE

1 TBSP BROWN SUGAR

2 TBSP HAZELNUT OIL

2 TSP RED WINE VINEGAR

4 SLICES OF WHOLEMEAL COUNTRY-STYLE BREAD, ABOUT 1CM THICK

2 TBSP DIJON MUSTARD

260G COOKED BEEF, THINLY SLICED

HANDFUL OF WATERCRESS, WASHED

SALT AND FRESHLY GROUND BLACK PEPPER

Put the shallots in a pan with the red wine and sugar, then simmer until the wine has completely evaporated. Set the shallots aside.

Whisk the hazelnut oil with the vinegar and season with salt and pepper to make a dressing.

Toast the bread on both sides, then spread mustard over one side of each slice. Add slices of beef and top with the sticky shallots. Toss the watercress with the dressing and serve with the tartines.

TARTINE SAUCISSON EMMENTAL
Salami & Cheese Open Sandwich

I've suggested sourdough bread and Emmental cheese here but any kind of bread will do, as long as it's good quality, and you can use oddments of cheese. You could also make mini versions of this recipe to serve as snacks or canapés.

Serves 2

2 SLICES OF SOURDOUGH, 1CM THICK

1 TBSP CHOPPED PARSLEY

5 CORNICHONS, CHOPPED

2 TBSP MAYONNAISE

6−8 THIN SLICES OF EMMENTAL CHEESE

6−8 SLICES OF SALAMI OR SAUCISSON SEC

LETTUCE LEAVES, WASHED

FRESHLY GROUND BLACK PEPPER

If the bread is super-fresh, there's no need to toast it. Otherwise, toast it lightly.

Mix the parsley and cornichons with the mayonnaise.

Arrange the cheese, salami or saucisson and lettuce leaves on the slices of bread. It's nice to curl the cheese and salami slices slightly to provide some height.

Dot the mayonnaise mixture over each tartine and season with a little black pepper.

TARTINE BRETONNE

Open Sandwich with Sardines & Red Onion

Canned sardines are held in high esteem in France and they're an excellent item to have in your store-cupboard. Some of the best are from Brittany and come with different oils and flavourings. You can also get great canned mussels, octopus, squid, oysters, mackerel and cod liver and they all make excellent tartines. Roscoff onions are extra-special onions grown in Brittany, but regular red onions are fine too.

Serves 4

4 SLICES OF BREAD, 1CM THICK (SOURDOUGH IS GOOD)

1 TBSP SALTED BRITTANY BUTTER

1 RED ONION OR OIGNON DE ROSCOFF

220G CANNED SARDINES OR OTHER SEAFOOD

HANDFUL OF LAMB'S LETTUCE (CORN SALAD), WASHED

60G SAMPHIRE, WASHED

1 TBSP WHITE WINE VINEGAR

Toast the bread on both sides and spread butter on one side of each slice. Slice the onion into super-fine rings.

Divide the ingredients between the slices of toast, arranging them to give a bit of height. Then drizzle with a little oil from the sardine can and some vinegar.

TARTINE CHÈVRE ET FIGUES

Open Sandwich with Goats' Cheese & Figs

Figs and goats' cheese go beautifully together and this open sandwich is popular in Provence. Goats' curd is a lovely fresh cheese that makes a good contrast with the stronger hard cheese.

Serves 4

4 TBSP EXTRA VIRGIN OLIVE OIL

4 SLICES OF BREAD, 1CM THICK (WALNUT BREAD IS PARTICULARLY NICE HERE)

6 FRESH FIGS, CUT INTO QUARTERS

2 TBSP CLEAR HONEY

3 TBSP GOATS' CURD

1 HARD GOATS' CHEESE (SUCH AS CROTTIN OR PÉLARDON), GRATED

HANDFUL OF ROCKET LEAVES, WASHED

FRESHLY GROUND BLACK PEPPER

Drizzle a little of the oil on to the slices of bread and grill them on a hot griddle pan until nicely charred on both sides.

Put the figs on a baking sheet and drizzle them with the honey. Place them under a hot grill until they're lightly caramelised.

Spoon the goats' curd on to the slices of griddled bread and divide the figs between them. Top with the grated hard cheese and the rocket leaves. Drizzle on the remaining olive oil and finish with a little pepper.

TARTINE NORMANDE

Open Sandwich with Cheese, Apples & Calvados

There are so many delicious cheeses from Normandy it's hard to choose between them, but the ones that I think work best for this dish are Camembert, Pont l'Evêque or Pavé d'Auge. Apples and cider are also a speciality of Normandy and are a perfect combination.

Serves 4

2 APPLES

2 TBSP BUTTER

1 TBSP SUGAR

100ML DRY CIDER

4 SLICES OF BREAD (SOURDOUGH IS BEST)

1 TBSP CRÈME FRAÎCHE

1 TBSP CALVADOS

200G CHEESE (SEE ABOVE), SLICED

HANDFUL OF BITTER SALAD LEAVES, WASHED

SALT AND FRESHLY GROUND BLACK PEPPER

Peel one of the apples and cut it into small wedges. Place the wedges in a hot pan with the butter and sugar and cook until caramelised, then add the cider and boil rapidly until the liquid has completely evaporated. Take the pan off the heat and set aside.

Toast the bread. Mix the crème fraîche with the calvados, then season with salt and pepper. Spread the mixture on to the slices of toast. Add slices of cheese, the cooked apple and salad leaves. Cut the remaining apple into fine matchsticks and sprinkle them on top.

TARTINE PROVENÇALE
Provençal Open Sandwich

With the flavours of Provence on an open sandwich, this tastes as good as it looks.

Serves 4

1 MEDIUM FENNEL BULB

1 TBSP OLIVE OIL

12 GOOD-QUALITY SALTED ANCHOVIES
IN OIL

4 SLICES OF BREAD, 1CM THICK
(SOURDOUGH OR A GOOD-QUALITY
BAGUETTE BOTH WORK WELL)

4 TBSP TAPENADE (SEE PAGE 30)

12 CHERRY TOMATOES, HALVED

HANDFUL OF ROCKET LEAVES, WASHED

2 TBSP TOMATO AND GARLIC PURÉE
(SEE PAGE 293)

ROCKET OR BASIL LEAVES, WASHED

SALT AND FRESHLY GROUND
BLACK PEPPER

Trim the fennel bulb and remove the outer leaves. Using a mandolin, slice the fennel lengthways into super-thin shavings. Place these in a bowl of iced water, leave them for 10 minutes and they will curl attractively.

Drain the fennel well, then dress it with the olive oil and season with salt and pepper. Drain the anchovies and cut them in half lengthways.

Lightly toast the bread and spread some tapenade on each slice. Add fennel, anchovies, tomatoes and rocket, arranging them in whatever order you like. Finish with dots of tomato and garlic purée and some basil leaves.

SALADES

Salads

Whether simply a bowl of perfectly seasoned leaves or a more elaborate salade composé, a fresh salad is an essential part of a French meal. I serve salad as a starter, an accompaniment to the main course or as a light lunch. In this chapter you will find ideas for beautiful salads to suit every occasion.

CONCOMBRE À LA CRÈME
Creamed Cucumber Salad

This was my grandmother's favourite salad and the flavours and texture are part of my childhood memories. The best cucumbers for this are the rough-skinned variety that have a slightly bitter edge to them. If possible, make the salad the day before and leave it in the fridge to allow the flavours to develop.

Serves 4

2 MEDIUM CUCUMBERS

2 TBSP COARSE SEA SALT

2 TBSP CRÈME FRAÎCHE

2 GARLIC CLOVES, PEELED AND FINELY CHOPPED

JUICE OF 1 LEMON

1 TBSP CHOPPED CURLY PARSLEY

FRESHLY GROUND BLACK PEPPER

Peel and core the cucumbers, then cut them crossways into slices about 5mm thick.

Put the slices in a colander with the coarse salt, mix and leave them to marinate for at least 30 minutes. The cucumber will give off quite a bit of water, so drain the slices well after marinating and press them to get rid of the moisture.

Mix the crème fraîche with the garlic and lemon juice in a bowl, then add the cucumber. Cover the bowl and leave the salad to chill in the fridge – overnight if possible. Just before serving, sprinkle the salad with chopped parsley and season it with black pepper.

SALADE VERTE

Green Salad

Probably the most commonly consumed dish in France, there are hundreds of combinations in the choice of leaves, let alone the dressing. Try to choose a good variety of leaves, some bitter, some sweet and fragrant, others tender or crunchy. The choice of herbs is really up to personal taste and availability. Here is a mixture that I particularly like. If you don't need this quantity of salad, just put the washed and dried leaves in a bag and store them in the fridge for another time. The dressing keeps well too.

Serves 8

1 ROUND LETTUCE

1 CURLY ENDIVE

1 ROMAINE LETTUCE

1 OAKLEAF LETTUCE

Dressing

80ML OLIVE OIL

2 TSP DIJON MUSTARD

1 TSP SALT

2 TBSP TARRAGON VINEGAR

1 TBSP CHOPPED PARSLEY

1 TBSP CHOPPED CHERVIL

1 SMALL BUNCH OF CHIVES SNIPPED

FRESHLY GROUND BLACK PEPPER

Pick over the salad leaves and discard any that are damaged. Wash them carefully in ice-cold water, then drain them and dry them thoroughly in a salad spinner. Put the leaves in a salad bowl.

Mix the dressing ingredients together in a small jug. Just before serving, add some dressing to the salad and toss well.

SALADE DE CÉLERI-RAVE, POMME ET ROQUEFORT

Celeriac, Apple & Roquefort Salad

We French love celeriac and this is a lighter, fresher dish than the traditional céleri rémoulade. These ingredients work well together and the cheese has a strong flavour so you only need a small amount.

Serves 4

500G CELERIAC, PEELED

1 TBSP RED WINE VINEGAR

2 TSP DIJON MUSTARD

4 TBSP OLIVE OIL

1 GREEN APPLE

JUICE OF 1 LEMON (OPTIONAL)

80G ROQUEFORT CHEESE, CRUMBLED

CELERY LEAVES

SALT AND FRESHLY GROUND
BLACK PEPPER

Cut the celeriac into super-thin matchsticks and put them in a bowl. Mix the vinegar, mustard and oil to make the dressing and season with salt and pepper, then fold this into the celeriac. Chill the celeriac in the fridge for a few hours or overnight.

Cut the apple into thin matchsticks. If you're not serving the salad right away, toss the apple in the lemon juice to stop it going brown. When you're ready to serve, add the apple and crumbled cheese to the salad and finish with some celery leaves.

CŒUR DE LAITUE MIMOSA
Lettuce Heart Mimosa

Mimosa refers to the topping of crumbled egg yolk and egg white scattered over a salad, said to resemble the spring flowers. This classic French salad is best made with round summer lettuce but it's also good with Little Gems at other times of year. Replacing some of the olive oil with vegetable oil and adding a little water to the dressing makes it lighter and less rich than the traditional version, but it's still creamy and delicious.

Serves 4

4 FREE-RANGE EGGS (AT ROOM TEMPERATURE)

4 ROUND LETTUCES OR LITTLE GEMS

SMALL BUNCH OF CHIVES, SNIPPED

Vinaigrette Dressing

1 TBSP DIJON MUSTARD

1 TBSP RED WINE VINEGAR

3 TBSP VEGETABLE OIL

1 TBSP OLIVE OIL

SALT AND FRESHLY GROUND BLACK PEPPER

Put the eggs in a pan of cold water, bring the water to the boil and cook for 9 minutes. Cool the eggs under running cold water, then shell them and cut them in half. Chop the yolks and whites and put them in separate bowls.

Put all the ingredients for the dressing in a jar with 2 tablespoons of water and shake well until emulsified.

Cut the lettuces in half and rinse them in cold water. Drain, then pat them dry.

Dress the lettuces with the vinaigrette and sprinkle over the chopped egg. Top with the snipped chives and serve at once.

CÉLERI RÉMOULADE
Celeriac Salad

This is a much-loved salad that you will find up and down France – in delis, in brasseries as a starter served with cured meats, and in Michelin-starred restaurants with truffle and smoked duck. It can be heavy if there's too much mayonnaise, so I like to use as little mayo as possible and add some crème fraîche. This salad is best kept in the fridge for 24 hours before serving.

Serves 6

1 CELERIAC (ABOUT 400G), PEELED

2 TBSP LIGHT MAYONNAISE (SEE BELOW)

2 TBSP CRÈME FRAÎCHE

1 TBSP WHOLEGRAIN MUSTARD

JUICE OF 1 LEMON

SALT AND FRESHLY GROUND BLACK PEPPER

Light Mayonnaise

1 FREE-RANGE EGG

1 TBSP DIJON MUSTARD

1 TBSP WHITE WINE VINEGAR OR LEMON JUICE

120G GREEK-STYLE YOGHURT

200ML SUNFLOWER OIL

Using a mandolin, cut the celeriac into fine matchsticks. You could grate the celeriac if you like, but I think it's nice to have the long matchsticks for texture.

Put the celeriac in a bowl, add the remaining ingredients and season with salt and pepper. Cover the bowl and put the salad in the fridge for 24 hours. This salad keeps well for up to a week.

LIGHT MAYONNAISE
Classic mayonnaise is made with egg yolks only, but I find using the white as well and adding some yoghurt makes a lighter sauce.

Crack the egg into a food processor, then add the mustard, vinegar and yoghurt. Season with salt and pepper. Start to blend, then begin drizzling in the oil until the mixture emulsifies.

SALADE DE FENOUIL, NOIX ET FIGUE

Fennel, Walnut & Fig Salad

This lovely fruity salad is one to make at the end of summer or in early autumn, when figs, grapes and walnuts are all in season. You can use wet walnuts (fresh walnuts that haven't been dried) if available. The grape juice makes an interesting dressing.

Serves 4

25 WHITE GRAPES

4 TBSP OLIVE OIL

1 LARGE FENNEL BULB, TRIMMED

JUICE OF 1 LEMON

2 FRESH FIGS

60G WALNUT KERNELS

1 TBSP CASTER SUGAR

LEAVES FROM A BUNCH OF BASIL

SALT AND FRESHLY GROUND
BLACK PEPPER

Crush the grapes or blitz them in a food processor, then put them in a fine sieve over a bowl and press well to collect the juice. Discard the pulp. Mix the juice with the olive oil and season with salt and pepper to make a dressing.

Slice the fennel as finely as possible, preferably with a mandolin, then toss the slices in lemon juice. Cut the figs into halves or quarters, depending on their size.

Put the walnuts in a dry frying pan with the sugar and cook them over a medium heat, tossing frequently, until the sugar melts and caramelises the nuts. Set them aside to cool.

Arrange the fennel slices and figs on a serving dish, add the dressing, then scatter the nuts and basil leaves on top. Serve at once.

SALADE DE BROCOLI GRILLÉ AUX AMANDES ET CITRON

Grilled Broccoli Salad with Almonds & Lemon

Tenderstem broccoli is best for this simple salad, but regular broccoli or even romanesco can be used – just cut it into small wedges.

Serves 4

2 UNWAXED LEMONS

2 TBSP CASTER SUGAR

80G FLAKED ALMONDS

80ML VEGETABLE OIL

250G TENDERSTEM BROCCOLI

PINCH OF SALT

PINCH OF PIMENT D'ESPELETTE (SEE PAGE 8) OR CHILLI FLAKES

Peel the lemons, then slice the peel into thin matchsticks. Put these in a pan, generously cover with cold water and bring to the boil. Drain and repeat this process twice more. The third time, add the sugar and simmer until the liquid is syrupy. Leave to cool, then drain the matchsticks and set them and the syrup aside. Squeeze the juice from the lemons and set it aside.

Toast the almonds in a dry pan until golden brown. Keep a close eye on them so they don't burn.

Drizzle some of the oil over the broccoli, then grill it on a griddle pan over a high heat, or on a barbecue, until well charred but still nice and crunchy.

Mix the lemon juice with the remaining oil, the syrup from preparing the lemon peel and a pinch of salt. Drizzle this over the grilled broccoli, then scatter the almonds on top, along with the cooked lemon peel. Dust with a little piment d'Espelette or some chilli flakes before serving.

SALADE DE CHAMPIGNONS À L'EMMENTAL ET HERBES

Mushroom Salad with Emmental & Herbs

To enjoy this salad to the full, be sure to use super-fresh, firm mushrooms, good fresh herbs and do not serve it straight from the fridge. Emmental is my cheese of choice for this recipe, but Gruyère would also be fine. The slices of cheese must be really thin, so use a mandolin or a cheese slicer.

Serves 4

220G MUSHROOMS

2 TBSP LEMON JUICE

1 GARLIC CLOVE, PEELED AND
FINELY CHOPPED

4 TBSP OLIVE OIL

2 TBSP CHOPPED PARSLEY

1 TBSP THYME LEAVES

1 TBSP ROUGHLY CHOPPED TARRAGON

1 TBSP SNIPPED BASIL

60G EMMENTAL CHEESE, VERY THINLY
SLICED

SALT AND FRESHLY GROUND
BLACK PEPPER

Wash the mushrooms and slice them really thinly. Put them in a bowl and toss them with the lemon juice, then season with salt and pepper.

Mix the finely chopped garlic with the oil and herbs, pour this mixture on to the mushrooms and toss everything well again.

Just before serving, add the slices of cheese on top of the salad.

SALADE DE COURGETTES ET OLIVES
Courgette Salad with Olives

Choose small courgettes, as they will be sweeter and have fewer seeds, and if possible use a mix of varieties and colours. I like to finish this salad with deep-fried courgette flowers but if you can't get them, don't worry. The salad will still be delicious.

Serves 4

400G MIXED COURGETTES

2 MEDIUM SHALLOTS, PEELED AND FINELY SLICED

1 TBSP HONEY

JUICE OF 1 LEMON AND ZEST OF ½

4 TBSP STRONG-FLAVOURED EXTRA VIRGIN OLIVE OIL

80G PITTED BLACK OLIVES, ROUGHLY CHOPPED

8 COURGETTE FLOWERS (OPTIONAL)

VEGETABLE OIL, FOR DEEP-FRYING (OPTIONAL)

POTATO FLOUR OR CORNFLOUR, FOR DUSTING (OPTIONAL)

SALT AND FRESHLY GROUND BLACK PEPPER

Using a sharp knife, cut the courgettes into different shapes – slices, matchsticks, dice, ribbons – to add interest to the salad. Put them in a bowl, season with salt and pepper and add the shallots.

Mix the honey with the lemon juice and zest, then add the olive oil and pour this dressing over the courgettes. Add the roughly chopped olives.

If using the flowers, cook them just before serving. Carefully open the flowers and remove the stamens, as they can be very bitter. Half-fill a deep-fat fryer with vegetable oil and heat to 180°C. Dust the flowers in a little potato flour or cornflour and deep-fry them for 2 minutes until crisp. Drain them carefully and season with a little salt, then put them on top of the salad and serve at once.

SALADE DE HARICOTS VERTS
French Bean Salad

Most green beans have had the strings bred out of them so no longer need to be trimmed both ends. My favourites are the super-fine beans known as 'aiguillette', but all green beans, such as bobby or runner beans, are great, including the yellow or purple varieties. I like to use a light olive oil or even a neutral vegetable oil for the dressing so it doesn't overpower the salad.

Serves 4

320G MIXED GREEN BEANS

Classic French Dressing

1 MEDIUM SHALLOT, PEELED AND FINELY CHOPPED (OPTIONAL)

60ML WHITE WINE VINEGAR

180ML LIGHT OLIVE OIL

1 TBSP DIJON MUSTARD

1 GARLIC CLOVE, FINELY CRUSHED (OPTIONAL)

SALT AND FRESHLY GROUND BLACK PEPPER

Pick over the beans and if using large beans, such as runner or bobby, slice them before cooking.

Bring a big pan of water to the boil and generously season with salt. Add the beans and cook them until tender. Depending on the variety you're using, this should take 4–6 minutes, but taste a bean to check. The beans for a salad should not be overcooked.

Once the beans are ready, drain and refresh them in a bowl of iced water. This halts the cooking process and also helps to keep the lovely green colour. Drain the beans again, then add 8 tablespoons of the dressing and serve warm or cold. Store the rest of the dressing in the fridge.

CLASSIC FRENCH DRESSING

If you are not keen on raw shallot, leave it out, likewise the garlic, but the following method of rinsing and marinating the shallot makes it mild and very digestible.

If using the chopped shallot, put it in a bowl, cover it with cold water and leave for 10 minutes. Drain, then rinse the shallot under cold running water. Put it back in the bowl, add the vinegar and leave to steep for 5–6 minutes, stirring a few times.

Add the rest of the ingredients, whisk them together and season with salt and pepper.

SALADE DE CHAMPIGNONS ET CÉLERI

Wild Mushroom & Celery Salad

Use seasonal wild mushrooms if possible, but cultivated oyster and shiitake are also fine, particularly if served warm. The dressing is made with Viandox which is a French yeast and beef extract seasoning. If you can't get any, Bovril is a good alternative.

Serves 4

4 CELERY STICKS

JUICE OF 1 LEMON

220G MIXED MUSHROOMS

4 TBSP OLIVE OIL

1 SHALLOT, PEELED AND CHOPPED

1 GARLIC CLOVE, PEELED AND CHOPPED

2 TBSP CHOPPED PARSLEY

1 TBSP VIANDOX OR BOVRIL

1 TBSP SHERRY VINEGAR

SALT AND FRESHLY GROUND BLACK PEPPER

Trim the celery, then cut each stick into 3. Bring a pan of salted water to the boil, add the lemon juice and cook the celery for 6–8 minutes until tender. Drain the celery and put it in a serving bowl.

Trim the mushrooms and wipe them clean. Heat a tablespoon of the oil in a pan and fry the mushrooms over a high heat until lightly browned. Add the shallot and garlic, season with salt and pepper, then cook for a further minute. Take the pan off the heat and add the parsley, then tip the mushrooms into a bowl with the cooked celery.

Mix the Viandox, or Bovril, with the rest of the oil and the vinegar. Pour this dressing on to the mushrooms and celery and serve.

SALADE TIÈDE D'OIGNONS NOUVEAUX ET SARRASIN

Warm Salad of New Season Onions & Buckwheat

I love the mild, sweet taste of new season onions, and the nuttiness of the buckwheat goes perfectly with them. You can also use the green tops of the onions in this really healthy, flavoursome salad. Spring onions are fine when new season onions are unavailable.

Serves 4

220G BUCKWHEAT

2 BAY LEAVES

350ML VEGETABLE STOCK

12−18 NEW SEASON ONIONS OR SHALLOTS, WITH GREEN TOPS

6 TBSP OLIVE OIL

2 TSP SUGAR

200ML WHITE WINE

4 TBSP TARRAGON LEAVES

1 TBSP RED WINE VINEGAR

SALT AND FRESHLY GROUND BLACK PEPPER

Put the buckwheat in a pan with the bay leaves and stock, then bring to the boil. Cover the pan, turn down the heat and leave the buckwheat to simmer gently for 25 minutes. Take the pan off the heat and set it aside, covered, for another 10 minutes, then season the buckwheat with salt and pepper.

Trim the green tops off the onions and set them aside. Cut the onions into halves or quarters, depending on their size. Heat a tablespoon of the olive oil in a frying pan, add the onions and cook them until lightly browned. Season them with salt and pepper, then add the sugar and the wine. Cover the pan and simmer for 5 minutes, then remove the lid. The onions should be cooked, but still have a little crunch, and the liquid should have almost evaporated.

Slice half of the green onion tops and mix them with the tarragon. Scatter the buckwheat on to a dish and add the onions, then sprinkle the greens and tarragon mixture on top. Mix the rest of the oil with the vinegar and season with salt and pepper, then drizzle this dressing over the salad before serving.

ÉPINARDS AUX LARD FUMÉS
Spinach & Smoked Bacon Salad

Choose the freshest baby leaf spinach you can find as you'll be eating it raw, and make sure you pat it dry thoroughly or the dressing won't coat the leaves. This makes an excellent side salad or you can add a poached egg for a delicious light lunch.

Serves 4

180G BABY LEAF SPINACH, WASHED

120G SMOKED BACON OR VENTRÈCHE (SEE PAGE 8), DICED

1 TSP DIJON MUSTARD

1 TBSP RED WINE VINEGAR

1 TBSP OLIVE OIL

1 SHALLOT, SLICED

FRESHLY GROUND BLACK PEPPER

Wash the spinach and dry it well, then pile it all into a salad bowl.

Put the diced bacon (or ventrèche) in a warm frying pan to render the fat, then gradually increase the temperature to crisp up the bacon. Take the pan off the heat, then add the mustard, vinegar and oil to make the dressing and season with pepper – you shouldn't need salt because of the salty bacon.

Pour the bacon and dressing mixture over the spinach and sprinkle the sliced shallot on top.

SALADE DE RIZ NIÇOISE
Rice Salad Niçoise

Canned tuna is perfect for this rice-based dish, which is a nice change from the classic Niçoise salad and makes a filling, nourishing lunch. Serve at room temperature for the best flavour.

Serves 4

200G LONG-GRAIN RICE

2 RED PEPPERS, CUT IN HALF

6 TBSP OLIVE OIL

2 TBSP RED WINE VINEGAR

4 SALTED ANCHOVIES, CHOPPED

1 TBSP CAPERS

300G CANNED TUNA IN OIL, DRAINED AND FLAKED

100G PITTED OLIVES (GREEN AND BLACK), ROUGHLY CHOPPED

2 SPRING ONIONS, THINLY SLICED

100G BABY SPINACH LEAVES, WASHED

SALT AND FRESHLY GROUND BLACK PEPPER

Put the rice in a pan with plenty of water. Add salt, then bring to the boil and cook the rice for 25 minutes or until tender. Drain the rice well and spread it out on a plate so it cools quickly.

Put the peppers, skin-side up, under a hot grill until blackened and charred. Leave them to cool, then peel off the skins and cut the flesh into thin strips. Discard the seeds and any white membrane.

Whisk the oil, vinegar, anchovies and capers together to make a dressing. Season with pepper and a little salt – not too much because of the anchovies.

Put the rice in a serving dish and add the flaked tuna, pepper strips, olives, spring onions and spinach leaves. Add the dressing just before serving and toss.

SOUPES ET POTAGES

Soups

For me, a good bowl of soup, perhaps with a salad, makes an ideal meal – light but filling, so a good healthy option. Most of the soups in this chapter are not as rich as the traditional versions, with less cream and butter. I like to keep my soups seasonal, cooking the heartier recipes, such as the garbure, in winter and the lighter options, such as watercress and crayfish, in the summer months.

VELOUTÉ D'ÉPINARDS

Spinach Soup

A vibrant, green soup that's full of goodness – what's not to like? You could add some
bacon or smoked chicken if you like, but for me, just some toasted bread with tapenade
(see page 30) or aïoli (see page 32) hits the spot with this.

Serves 4

200G POTATOES, PEELED AND DICED

1 WHITE ONION, PEELED AND
CHOPPED

1 GARLIC CLOVE, PEELED AND
CHOPPED

GRATING OF NUTMEG

300G SPINACH, WASHED

4 TBSP OLIVE OIL

SALT AND FRESHLY GROUND
BLACK PEPPER

Put the potatoes, onion and garlic in a pan, add 600ml
of water and place over a medium heat . Season with
salt, pepper and a grating of nutmeg, then simmer until
the potatoes are cooked.

Add the spinach and stir it in, then simmer for 5
minutes. Stir in the oil, then blitz the soup in a food
processor or blender until smooth.

POTAGE CULTIVATEUR

Vegetable Soup

Traditionally, there should be a little pork fat or bacon in this hearty soup, but I find it lighter without and still very delicious. I dice the vegetables neatly for this recipe, as I think it is nice to keep it chunky rather than blitzed. You can vary the ingredients and use different root vegetables and greens, depending on what's in season.

Serves 6

4 TBSP VEGETABLE OIL

1 LEEK, CLEANED AND CHOPPED

250G CABBAGE, FINELY CHOPPED

2 CARROTS, PEELED AND CUT INTO 1CM DICE

2 TURNIPS, PEELED AND CUT INTO 1CM DICE

200G POTATOES, PEELED AND CUT INTO 1CM DICE

2 CELERY STICKS, DICED

1 BOUQUET GARNI (SEE PAGE 8)

3 LITRES VEGETABLE STOCK (OR WATER)

4 TBSP CHOPPED PARSLEY

SALT AND FRESHLY GROUND BLACK PEPPER

Heat the oil in a large pan. Add the vegetables and cook them gently for 10 minutes, stirring regularly. Do not allow them to colour.

Add the bouquet garni, season with salt and pepper, then pour in the vegetable stock – or you can use water. Bring to the boil and then gently simmer the soup for 20 minutes to reduce the liquid. Sprinkle over the chopped parsley and serve.

CRÈME DUBARRY
Cauliflower Soup

Classic recipes for this indulgent French soup often include cream, but I find that just using milk as well as stock keeps it lighter but still gives a lovely velvety texture. Adding the raw cauliflower at the end provides intense flavour and I love the mixture of colours and textures. If you can't find golden or purple cauliflower you could use more of the ordinary white cauliflower or some broccoli or romanesco.

Serves 6

½ LARGE CAULIFLOWER (ABOUT 500G)

2 TBSP BUTTER

1 MEDIUM POTATO, PEELED AND THINLY SLICED

1 LEEK (WHITE PART ONLY), CLEANED AND THINLY SLICED

500ML MILK

500ML VEGETABLE STOCK

GRATING OF NUTMEG

200G PURPLE AND/OR GOLDEN CAULIFLOWER

2 TBSP OLIVE OIL

½ TBSP RED WINE VINEGAR

SALT AND FRESHLY GROUND BLACK PEPPER

Chop the cauliflower into small pieces, stalks included.

Melt the butter in a large pan and add the cauliflower, potato and leek. Cook them gently over a medium heat for 15 minutes but don't allow them to colour.

Season the vegetables with salt and pepper, then add the milk, stock and a grating of nutmeg. Bring the soup to a simmer and cook for 20 minutes, then blitz in a food processor or blender until smooth. Pass the soup through a fine sieve.

Cut the coloured cauliflower into little florets. Season them with oil, vinegar and a touch of salt and then sprinkle some over each serving.

SOUPE DE TOMATES
Roasted Tomato Soup

Roasting the tomatoes concentrates their flavour beautifully and this is still an easy soup to make. I like to use plum or Roma tomatoes but any kind will do. The anchovies add depth of flavour and umami, but if you don't want to include them, adjust the seasoning. Serve the soup with pistou (see page 288) or a drizzle of olive oil to enrich.

Serves 6

18 TOMATOES

2 RED ONIONS, PEELED AND THICKLY SLICED

4 GARLIC CLOVES, PEELED AND THICKLY SLICED

1 MEDIUM RED CHILLI, CUT IN HALF

1 TBSP THYME LEAVES

4 TBSP OLIVE OIL

6 ANCHOVY FILLETS

1.8 LITRES VEGETABLE STOCK

SALT AND FRESHLY GROUND BLACK PEPPER

Preheat the oven to 200°C/Fan 180°C/Gas 6. Cut the tomatoes in half and place them in a big bowl with the onions, garlic, chilli and thyme leaves. Add the oil and toss well to coat the tomatoes. Scatter the contents of the bowl into a large roasting tin, making sure the tomatoes aren't too crowded together.

Roast the tomatoes in the oven for 1 hour, stirring them a couple of times. The tomatoes should take on some charred edges and give off a lot of moisture. Pour everything, juices and all, into a pan, then add the anchovies and stock and place over a medium heat.

Season with salt and pepper, bring to a simmer and cook for 20 minutes, then blitz the soup in a blender or food processor until smooth. For a really silky finish, pass the soup through a fine sieve.

GARBURE
Ham & Vegetable Soup

A great one-pot dish and a meal in itself, garbure is a thick hearty soup from South-west France. This version is made with ham, but you can also use duck or some of each. It's best cooked a few days before you want to serve it to give the flavours a chance to mature – and don't forget to soak the beans the night before making the soup.

Serves 6

160G DRIED WHITE BEANS

1 SMOKED HAM HOCK (ABOUT 750G)

1 THYME SPRIG

1 BAY LEAF

4 TBSP OLIVE OIL OR PORK FAT

2 CARROTS, PEELED AND DICED

2 POTATOES, PEELED AND DICED

2 LEEKS (WHITE AND PALE GREEN), CLEANED AND FINELY CHOPPED

2 ONIONS, PEELED AND FINELY CHOPPED

6 GARLIC CLOVES, PEELED AND CRUSHED

1 SMALL SAVOY CABBAGE, SHREDDED

SALT AND FRESHLY GROUND BLACK PEPPER

Soak the beans in plenty of cold water overnight.

Place the ham hock in a large pan with the thyme and bay leaf. Add cold water to cover, bring to the boil, then turn the heat down to a gentle simmer. Cover the pan with a loose-fitting lid and leave the hock to simmer until the meat is tender and falling off the bone. This usually takes about 2½ hours – top up with boiling water if necessary.

Leave the ham hock to cool in the pan, then drain it and reserve the liquid. Pick all the meat off the bone and shred it, then dice the skin and set it all aside.

Warm the oil or pork fat in a pan, add the vegetables and cook them gently until tender. Pour in the reserved cooking liquid and the drained beans, then season and bring to the boil. Turn the heat down and simmer for 1 hour. Stir in the shredded ham and diced skin, then serve the soup piping hot.

SOUPE AU LAIT ET VERMICELLES

Vermicelli Soup

This soup reminds me of my childhood. My mother used to make it if one of us wasn't feeling well or whenever something warm and comforting was needed. It always hit the spot for me and I still find myself making a bowl of this soup when there's not much in the fridge. It's quick and easy to prepare and you can use any kind of pasta, but 'angel hair' vermicelli works best.

Serves 2

1 TBSP BUTTER

1 ONION, PEELED AND FINELY CHOPPED OR GRATED

60G VERMICELLI

500ML MILK

80G GRUYÈRE, EMMENTAL, COMTÉ OR CANTAL CHEESE, GRATED

SALT AND FRESHLY GROUND BLACK PEPPER

Melt the butter in a pan, add the onion and cook it gently for 5–6 minutes without allowing it to colour. Add 500ml of water, season with salt and pepper, then bring to the boil. Add the vermicelli or other pasta.

Simmer until the pasta is tender, then add the milk and grated cheese, then bring back to a simmer. Take the pan off the heat and serve the soup at once.

VELOUTÉ DE POIS CHICHES ET HARISSA

Chickpea & Harissa Soup

It's fine to use canned chickpeas and ready-made harissa to make this a really quick soup – it tastes just as good. It's a nourishing, hearty dish and great served hot on a chilly winter day but also good cold.

Serves 6

400G CAN OF CHICKPEAS, DRAINED AND RINSED

1 MEDIUM ONION, PEELED AND CHOPPED

1 BAY LEAF

PINCH OF SALT

100ML GOOD OLIVE OIL

JUICE OF 2 LEMONS AND ZEST OF 1

SMALL BUNCH EACH OF CORIANDER, MINT AND FLATLEAF PARSLEY

1 TBSP HARISSA PASTE

SALT

Put the chickpeas in a pan and cover them with cold water, then add the chopped onion and bay leaf. Season with salt, bring to a simmer and leave to cook for about 10 minutes.

Remove the bay leaf, add 3 tablespoons of the oil and half the lemon juice, then blitz the soup in a blender or food processor until smooth.

Pick the leaves from the bunches of coriander, mint and parsley and rinse them in iced water. Dress them with a little of the olive oil, the rest of the lemon juice and the lemon zest. Mix the harissa with the remaining oil.

Pour the soup into bowls, drizzle over as much harissa as you like and top each bowlful with some herb salad.

SOUPE DE POMMES DE TERRE VIOLETTES

Purple Potato Soup

This is such a simple soup and is very quick and easy to make. You can, of course, use any kind of potato but the purple variety not only makes this soup a vibrant and unusual colour but also gives it a delicious, slightly nutty flavour.

Serves 6

1 TBSP BUTTER

1 LEEK (WHITE PART ONLY), CLEANED AND THINLY SLICED

750G POTATOES (VIOLETTA, PURPLE MAJESTY, PERUVIAN PURPLE OR EDZELL BLUE), PEELED AND DICED

1 BOUQUET GARNI (SEE PAGE 8)

1.5 LITRES CHICKEN OR VEGETABLE STOCK

GRATING OF NUTMEG

4 TBSP SINGLE CREAM

SALT AND FRESHLY GROUND BLACK PEPPER

Melt the butter in a large pan, add the leek and sweat it until softened but not browned.

Add the potatoes, bouquet garni and stock, then season well with salt, pepper and a grating of nutmeg. Simmer for 20 minutes or until the potatoes are soft. Remove the bouquet garni and blitz the soup in a blender or food processor until smooth.

Serve with a little cream drizzled on top of each serving.

POTAGE DE MAÏS ET CREVETTES GRISES

Sweetcorn & Brown Shrimp Soup

This is a light but satisfying soup. You only need a little crème fraîche but it adds a nice touch of acidity to offset the naturally sweet sweetcorn.

Serves 6

6 CORN ON THE COB

2 TBSP VEGETABLE OIL

2 ONIONS, PEELED AND THINLY SLICED

GRATING OF NUTMEG

3 TBSP CRÈME FRAÎCHE

120G PEELED BROWN SHRIMPS

SMOKED PAPRIKA

SALT AND FRESHLY GROUND
BLACK PEPPER

Remove the husks from the cobs. Take 4 of the cobs and carefully cut off the kernels with a knife and set them aside. Rub a little oil over the remaining 2 cobs and grill them on a hot griddle pan until cooked and nicely charred. Leave them to cool and then cut off the kernels and set them aside separately.

Heat the remaining oil in a pan and gently cook the onions and raw corn kernels. Once they are soft, add enough water to cover the vegetables by 3–4cm and season with salt, pepper and nutmeg. Bring to a simmer and cook for 20 minutes. Add the crème fraîche and blitz the soup in a blender or food processor until smooth. If you want an extra-smooth soup, pass it through a fine sieve.

Divide the shrimp between warm bowls, then pour the hot soup over them. Sprinkle the charred corn kernels on top and add a little smoked paprika.

SOUPE DE CHICONS ET MIMOLETTE
Chicory Soup with Mimolette Cheese

The Flanders region of northeast France is famous for its chicory (chicons) and deliciously nutty-tasting aged Mimolette cheese. The cheese is perfect in this soup and you only need a small amount per person so the dish isn't too rich. Mimolette does have a particularly good flavour but if you can't get any, use an aged Edam.

Serves 4

6 HEADS OF CHICORY (RED AND WHITE IF POSSIBLE)

1 TBSP VEGETABLE OIL

1 MEDIUM ONION, PEELED AND CHOPPED

1 GARLIC CLOVE, PEELED AND CHOPPED

1 LARGE POTATO, PEELED AND DICED

300ML BEER (FRUIT BEER IS BEST, SUCH AS KRIEK OR GUEUZE FRAMBOISE)

2 TBSP CRÈME FRAÎCHE

100G AGED MIMOLETTE CHEESE, CUT INTO THIN SHAVINGS

SALT AND FRESHLY GROUND BLACK PEPPER

Separate the chicory leaves and chop them, reserving 8 to garnish the soup. Slice these leaves lengthways and put them in a bowl of iced water so they curl up nicely.

Heat the oil in a pan and gently cook the chopped endive, onion and garlic until softened. Add the potato and cook for 20 minutes until it starts to colour. Pour in the beer and bring it to the boil, then add 400ml of water and season with salt and pepper. Simmer the soup for 20 minutes, then blitz it in a blender or food processor until smooth.

Stir in the crème fraiche and serve the hot soup in bowls, garnished with the reserved endive leaves and thin shavings of Mimolette cheese.

SOUPE DE FENOUIL ET ROUGET
Fennel Soup with Red Mullet

Fennel and red mullet were made for each other – their flavours go together perfectly.
If mullet is not available, this soup is also good made with gilthead bream.

Serves 4

2 FENNEL BULBS

4 TBSP OLIVE OIL

1 MEDIUM WHITE ONION,
PEELED AND FINELY CHOPPED

60ML WHITE VERMOUTH

2 TBSP PASTIS

1 LITRE VEGETABLE STOCK

1 TBSP PLAIN FLOUR

1 TBSP POWDERED ANISEED

4 FILLETS OF RED MULLET

SALT AND FRESHLY GROUND
BLACK PEPPER

Trim the fennel, then chop it into small pieces. Keep the fronds for garnishing the soup.

Heat a tablespoon of the oil in a large pan, add the fennel and the onion, and season with salt and pepper. When the fennel and onion are soft, add the vermouth and pastis, cook for 2 minutes, then add the stock. Bring to the boil and simmer for 10 minutes. Tip everything into a food processor and blitz until smooth.

Mix the flour and aniseed together and season with salt and pepper. Dust the mullet fillets with the flour. Heat a tablespoon of oil in a non-stick pan and fry the fillets until golden and just cooked.

Serve the soup in bowls and top with a piece of fish. Garnish with the fennel fronds and drizzle with the remaining olive oil.

SOUPE DE CRESSON ET ÉCREVISSES
Watercress & Crayfish Soup

As a child, I used to go gathering wild watercress and fishing for crayfish with my parents so this soup reminds me of those days. Crayfish, by the way, are small freshwater crustaceans, related to lobsters. This is a tasty and nutritious soup, with only a tiny amount of cream added to each serving.

Serves 6

1 TBSP BUTTER, PLUS EXTRA FOR CRAYFISH

1 ONION, PEELED AND THINLY SLICED

1 LARGE POTATO, PEELED AND THINLY SLICED

400G WATERCRESS, WASHED

1.4 LITRES JUST-BOILED WATER

300G CRAYFISH (COOKED OR RAW)

3 TBSP SINGLE CREAM

SALT AND FRESHLY GROUND BLACK PEPPER

Melt the tablespoon of butter in a pan and gently cook the onion and potato until soft, stirring frequently. Turn up the heat, add the watercress and season with salt and pepper, then pour in the water.

Bring the water back to the boil and simmer for 3–5 minutes. Blitz the soup in a blender or food processor until smooth, then pass it through a fine sieve.

If you are using cooked crayfish, crack them open and gently heat them through in a pan with a little butter. Divide them between the soup bowls, then add the hot soup and a small drizzle of cream.

If you are cooking your own crayfish, bring a large pan of salted water to the boil. Add the crayfish, cover the pan and bring back to the boil. Cook for 3 minutes, then drain. When the crayfish are cool enough to handle, remove the shells and serve as before. Keep the crayfish shells for making a stock or sauce.

VELOUTÉ DE VOLAILLE, CROQUETTE AU FROMAGE ET TRUFFE

Chicken Soup with Cheese Croquettes & Truffle

This is a thoroughly indulgent dish, one of those that can't be pared down, but it's well worth doing for a special treat. The only real extravagance is the truffle, which you don't have to include. Chicken wings are cheap and there's no need for the best Camembert here – in fact, you could use trimmings of any kind of cheese.

Serves 4

6 JOINTED CHICKEN WINGS, CLEANED AND TRIMMED

125ML WHITE WINE

1 THYME SPRIG

6 BUTTON MUSHROOMS, WIPED AND SLICED

1 LITRE WHITE CHICKEN STOCK

250G COOKED FLOURY POTATOES

2 FREE-RANGE EGGS

100G CAMEMBERT OR SIMILAR, DICED

2 TBSP FLOUR

2 TBSP BREADCRUMBS

VEGETABLE OIL, FOR DEEP-FRYING

2 TBSP CRÈME FRAÎCHE

100ML DOUBLE CREAM

1 TRUFFLE (OPTIONAL)

SALT AND FRESHLY GROUND BLACK PEPPER

Place the wings in a pan with the wine, thyme, mushrooms and stock. Bring to the boil and leave to simmer for 30 minutes. Strain the stock into a large bowl and put the wings on a plate. Weigh them down with something heavy to flatten them, then put them in the fridge to chill.

Pour the strained stock back into the pan and boil it until reduced by a third, then set aside. This is the chicken soup. Remove the bones from the chicken wings and cook the meat on a hot griddle until nice and crisp. Set them aside.

Mash the potatoes well, preferably with a potato ricer, then add one of the eggs and the cheese. Mix well, then roll the mixture into balls or cylinders. You can make 8 small croquettes or 4 larger ones. Beat the remaining egg in a bowl and put the flour and breadcrumbs on separate plates. Coat each croquette in flour, then dip it into beaten egg, and finally into the breadcrumbs.

Half-fill a large pan or a deep-fat fryer with vegetable oil and heat to 180°C. Deep-fry the croquettes for a couple of minutes until golden brown.

Reheat the soup, add the crème fraîche and cream, then season. Serve the soup in bowls with a griddled wing and a croquette or two. If you do have a truffle, add a few shavings to each bowl just before serving.

LÉGUMES, LÉGUMINEUSES ET CÉRÉALES

Vegetables, Pulses & Grains

Many people think of French food as protein led — meat or fish with vegetables simply as a garnish. That may still be true of some restaurant food, but the modern way is for vegetables, grains and pulses to be a hugely important part of the diet. There is a great market culture in France and people like buying seasonal produce that's been grown locally and picked when at its best.

CAVIAR D'AUBERGINE FUMÉE
Smoked Aubergine Purée

Aubergine dishes can be rather heavy and oily, but cooking the aubergines whole like this means that you don't need lots of oil but the result is still smooth and delicious. Serve the purée with crudités or croutons as a snack or an appetiser.

Serves 6-8

4 AUBERGINES

8 GARLIC CLOVES, WHOLE AND UNPEELED

JUICE OF 1 LEMON

1 TSP PIMENT D'ESPELETTE (SEE PAGE 8) OR CHILLI FLAKES

4 TBSP OLIVE OIL

1 SPRING ONION, FINELY CHOPPED

SALT

Place the whole aubergines, without any oil, in an ovenproof cast-iron pan or on a griddle.

Place the pan over a high heat and roast the aubergines until the skins are charred, turning them regularly so they blacken on all sides. This gives them a good smoky flavour. Preheat the oven to 220°C/Fan 200°C/Gas 7.

Add the garlic cloves and put the pan in the oven for 20 minutes. Remove and leave the aubergines and garlic to cool.

Cut the aubergines in half and scoop out all the flesh, scraping the skins to remove as much as possible. Peel the garlic.

Put the aubergine flesh and garlic in a food processor, add the lemon juice, piment d'espelette or chilli flakes and the oil, then season with salt. Blitz to a smooth texture, then tip the mixture into a bowl and stir in the spring onion.

AUBERGINE FARCIE PROVENÇALE
Stuffed Aubergines Provençal

A sauce made of red, yellow and green peppers keeps this baked aubergine dish really juicy and tasty but still light, as you only need a small amount of oil. Great on its own or served with a spoonful of pistou (see page 288).

Serves 4

2 MEDIUM AUBERGINES

2 GARLIC CLOVES, PEELED

2 TBSP OLIVE OIL

2 RED PEPPERS, CUT IN HALF

1 YELLOW PEPPER, CUT IN HALF

1 GREEN PEPPER, CUT IN HALF

1 TSP FENNEL SEEDS

1 TSP THYME LEAVES

SQUEEZE OF LEMON JUICE

SALT AND FRESHLY GROUND
BLACK PEPPER

Preheat the oven to 200°C/Fan 180°C/Gas 6. Cut the aubergines in half, lengthways, then score the flesh about 1cm deep in a criss-cross pattern.

Cut the garlic into thick slices and push these into the cuts in the aubergine halves. Brush the cut sides of the aubergine with a little of the oil.

Heat a pan on the hob. Season the aubergines well and place them cut-side down in the hot pan. Once the flesh is golden, turn the aubergines and place them cut-side up in an ovenproof dish. Put them in the oven and bake for 30 minutes.

Put the peppers, skin-side up, under a hot grill until blackened and charred. Leave them to cool, then peel off the skins and cut the flesh into strips about 5mm thick. Discard the seeds and any white membrane.

Heat the remaining oil in a pan and fry the strips of pepper, then add the fennel seeds, thyme and lemon juice. Season and spread the mixture over the aubergines. Serve hot or warm.

COULIS DE TOMATES
Tomato Coulis

I make loads of this in the summer, when tomatoes are at their cheapest and best, and serve it with dishes such as grilled fish or meat. Choose tomatoes that are really ripe and flavoursome for the best results and freeze some coulis in little tubs or bags for the winter months.

Makes 1 litre

1KG RIPE TOMATOES

2 TBSP OLIVE OIL

2 GARLIC CLOVES, PEELED AND CHOPPED

1 SHALLOT, PEELED AND CHOPPED

2 TSP TOMATO PASTE

1 THYME SPRIG

1 BAY LEAF

2 TSP SUGAR

SALT AND FRESHLY GROUND BLACK PEPPER

Remove the stalks from the tomatoes, cut the tomatoes in half and squeeze out the seeds. It doesn't matter if a few seeds remain, but you do want to get rid of excess moisture. Roughly chop the flesh.

Heat the olive oil in a pan and gently cook the chopped garlic and shallot for 5 minutes, stirring frequently. Don't let them brown. Add the tomato paste and herbs to the pan, cook for a further 2–3 minutes, then add the fresh tomatoes and sugar. Season with salt and pepper.

Cover the pan and leave to simmer for 30 minutes. Remove the herbs, then blitz the mixture to a fine purée in a food processor. If you want a really fine coulis, pass it through a sieve.

ARTICHAUTS FARCIS
Stuffed Artichokes

Globe artichokes do take a little while to prepare but they're well worth the effort.
These are stuffed with ham and eggs to make a light and elegant dish.

Serves 4

4 LARGE GLOBE ARTICHOKES

JUICE OF 1 LEMON

8 THIN SLICES OF BAYONNE HAM (SEE
PAGE 8) OR OTHER AIR-DRIED HAM

4 SMALL FREE-RANGE EGGS

4 TBSP DOUBLE CREAM

SALT AND FRESHLY GROUND
BLACK PEPPER

Prepare the artichokes. Snap the stalk off each one and pull off the first leaves from the base. Using a knife, trim off 2 layers of leaves and cut the base flat.

Bring a large pan of water to the boil and add salt. Then add the artichokes and lemon juice and cook for 25 minutes or until a skewer easily pierces the centre of the artichoke. Drain the artichokes and turn them bottom up to dry and cool.

When the artichokes are cold, carefully pull out the centre leaves to reveal the choke, then remove the choke from each one with a spoon. Run the artichokes under a tap to rinse them clean and get rid of any remaining bits of choke.

Preheat the oven to 180°C/Fan 160°C/Gas 4. Line the cavity of an artichoke with 2 slices of ham, then carefully crack in an egg and add a tablespoon of cream and a little black pepper. Repeat with the remaining artichokes and ingredients.

Place the filled artichokes in a roasting tin and add just-boiled water to a depth of 1cm. Bake the artichokes for 20 minutes – the egg yolks should still be runny. Serve immediately.

ASPERGES GRILLÉES AUX NOISETTES

Grilled Asparagus with Hazelnuts

A lovely vegetable dish to serve as a starter or with grilled fish, this is a real celebration of asparagus. It's best made with medium-sized green spears.

Serves 4

1 RED ONION, PEELED

28 GREEN ASPARAGUS SPEARS

2 TBSP OLIVE OIL

100G HAZELNUTS, SKINNED

4 TBSP HAZELNUT OIL

1 TBSP RED WINE VINEGAR

SALT AND FRESHLY GROUND BLACK PEPPER

Slice the onion into very fine rings. Place the rings in a bowl of cold water and leave them to soak for 20 minutes, then drain. This removes the harsh raw flavour of the onion.

Snap off the woody base of each asparagus spear and peel the stems if you think it necessary. Toss the asparagus in the oil to coat all over, then season with a little salt and pepper.

Heat a griddle pan or a barbecue and cook the asparagus on all sides until charred and tender. It shouldn't take more than about 5 minutes – the asparagus should still have a little bite. Set it aside and keep it warm.

Put the hazelnuts in a dry pan and cook them over a medium heat until golden. Keep them moving, as they will burn quite easily otherwise.

Once the nuts are toasted, place them in a food processor and add the hazelnut oil and vinegar. Season well and blitz to make a coarse paste.

Drizzle some of the hazelnut mixture over the asparagus and scatter the drained onion slices on top. Serve warm.

LÉGUMES, LÉGUMINEUSES ET CÉRÉALES • VEGETABLES, PULSES & GRAINS

ASPERGES, TOMATES ET ARTICHAUTS

Asparagus, Tomatoes & Artichokes

This is a recipe to make in spring when the first asparagus and baby artichokes make their appearance. Delicious and full of goodness, it celebrates the coming of a new season. Best enjoyed as a stand-alone dish.

Serves 6

12 BABY ARTICHOKES (POIVRADE OR VIOLET)

3 TBSP OLIVE OIL, PLUS EXTRA FOR DRIZZLING

1 SMALL ONION, CHOPPED

2 GARLIC CLOVES, CHOPPED

JUICE OF 1 LEMON

60ML DRY WHITE WINE

250ML VEGETABLE STOCK

200ML TOMATO PULP (CANNED CHOPPED TOMATOES OR PASSATA)

8 SALTED ANCHOVIES, ROUGHLY CHOPPED

600G GREEN ASPARAGUS SPEARS

BUNCH OF CHIVES, SNIPPED

SALT AND FRESHLY GROUND BLACK PEPPER

Peel the artichokes and cut them into quarters. Then cut off the excess hard leaves and remove the choke from each one.

Heat 2 tablespoons of the oil in a frying pan and fry the artichokes until they are lightly coloured. Add a little more oil, then reduce the heat, add the onion and garlic and cook them until soft.

Add the lemon juice and wine to the pan, partially cover with a lid and simmer for 2–3 minutes. Add the stock and tomato pulp and simmer for another 10 minutes, then add the anchovies and a generous amount of black pepper.

Snap off the woody base of each asparagus spear and peel the stems if you think it necessary. Bring a pan of salted water to the boil and cook the asparagus until it is tender and the point of a knife goes in easily. Cut each asparagus spear in half and add them to the pan with the artichokes and tomato, then reheat gently.

Serve drizzled with a little oil and garnished with snipped chives.

TOMATES À LA PROVENÇALE
Baked Tomatoes Provençal

This is my go-to accompaniment dish through the summer and autumn when tomatoes are at their best. I like to use Marmande or Oxheart but any kind of tomato will do. In the traditional recipe the tomatoes are just baked with the topping, but in my new version I caramelise them first to concentrate the wonderful flavour.

Serves 4

4 MEDIUM TOMATOES

SUGAR

2 TBSP OLIVE OIL

3 GARLIC CLOVES, PEELED AND CHOPPED

2 TBSP BREADCRUMBS

1 TBSP CHOPPED PARSLEY

1 TBSP THYME LEAVES

SALT AND FRESHLY GROUND BLACK PEPPER

Preheat the oven to 200°C/Fan 180°C/Gas 6. Cut the tomatoes in half and sprinkle them with a little sugar.

Heat a tablespoon of oil in a non-stick pan. When the pan is very hot, place the tomatoes cut-side down in the pan. Do not move them. Leave them to caramelise for about 3 minutes, then remove them and place them cut-side up in an ovenproof dish. Season with salt and black pepper.

Mix the garlic, breadcrumbs, parsley and thyme together and spread the mixture over the tomatoes. Drizzle over the remaining oil and bake the tomatoes in the oven for 15 minutes.

ENDIVE RÔTIE AU CITRON

Seared Chicory with Lemon

I like the slightly bitter taste of chicory, or endive as it also called, and it goes well with the sweet and sharp juices in this recipe. Serve this hot or cold, as an accompaniment to fish or as a stand-alone dish.

Serves 4

1 LARGE LEMON

4 LARGE HEADS OF CHICORY

2 TBSP OLIVE OIL

JUICE OF 1 ORANGE

2 TSP SUGAR

2 TBSP CHOPPED PARSLEY (OPTIONAL)

SALT AND FRESHLY GROUND
BLACK PEPPER

Peel the lemon as thinly as possible and cut the peel into thin matchsticks. Put them in a small saucepan and add cold water to cover, then bring the water to the boil. Drain and repeat. Cut the lemon flesh into segments, holding it over a bowl to collect any juice.

Cut each head of chicory into quarters lengthways. Sear them in a very hot frying pan with a small amount of the oil until golden on all sides. Remove them from the pan and set aside.

Place the strips of lemon peel in the frying pan. Add the orange juice, any juice from the lemon and the sugar, place the pan over a medium heat and simmer for a couple of minutes.

Add the seared chicory and the remaining oil and season with salt and pepper. Simmer the chicory while basting with the juice and oil until the liquid is reduced and sticky. Fold in the lemon segments and chopped parsley, if using, and serve hot or cold.

LÉGUMES, LÉGUMINEUSES ET CÉRÉALES • VEGETABLES, PULSES & GRAINS

POMMES NOUVELLES SAUTÉES
Sautéed New Potatoes

These potatoes are not fried, but sautéed and the way I cook them you really don't need a lot of fat. It's all about temperature control. You brown the potatoes in oil first over a high heat, then cook them more gently over a lower heat to give flavour and crispness. These are good with fish or meat or just on their own!

Serves 4

240G NEW POTATOES

8 GARLIC CLOVES, UNPEELED

GOOD PINCH OF SALT

1 TBSP VEGETABLE OIL

1 TBSP BUTTER

1 THYME SPRIG

Scrub the potatoes well and place them in a pan with the garlic cloves and a good pinch of salt. Add water to cover, then bring to the boil and simmer the potatoes for 2–3 minutes.

Drain the potatoes and when they are cool enough to handle, cut them in half. Set the garlic aside.

Heat the oil in a frying pan and cook the potatoes over a high heat until browned, then flip them over. Turn the heat down and add the garlic, butter and thyme. Cook the potatoes for 15 minutes or until tender, tossing them frequently.

ORGE PERLÉ ET NAVETS NOUVEAUX

Pearl Barley with Baby Turnips

Pearl barley is a wholesome and nutritious carb with lots of fibre so it keeps you full for longer! This dish is a healthy bowl of goodness and delicious just on its own. I love that you can use the whole turnip, including the leaves.

Serves 4

400G PEARL BARLEY

1.2 LITRES VEGETABLE STOCK

2 GARLIC CLOVES, PEELED AND CHOPPED

1 ONION, PEELED AND CHOPPED

16 BABY TURNIPS WITH TOPS

1 TBSP DIJON MUSTARD

6 ANCHOVY FILLETS

150ML OLIVE OIL

SALT AND FRESHLY GROUND BLACK PEPPER

Rinse the barley, place it in a pan with the stock and add the garlic, onion and a little seasoning. Bring the stock to a simmer and cook for 30 minutes by which time the barley should be tender. If it is still a little firm, add some hot water and continue to cook until done.

Trim off the turnip tops and set them aside, then wash the turnips. Bring a big pan of salted water to the boil, add the turnips and cook them until tender.

Wash the turnip tops and place half of them in a blender. Add the mustard, anchovy fillets, olive oil and 4 ice cubes, then blitz to a rough pesto-like paste. The ice helps the mixture to emulsify and keep the lovely fresh green colour.

Serve the barley and turnips in deep plates and drizzle the turnip top mixture on top.

CANELÉS DE LÉGUMES
Vegetable Cakes

These savoury versions of the traditional little Bordeaux cakes known as canelés are a real treat. They're packed with vegetables, so reasonably healthy, and they keep well for a couple of days. I like to make small ones for snacks or larger ones to serve as a meal. The traditional moulds are copper and need to be well buttered, but modern silicone moulds are much more practical and don't need any greasing. You can also use muffin tins for the large canelés.

Makes 10 big or 30 small

560ML MILK

50G BUTTER

160G CARROTS, PEELED AND DICED

GRATING OF NUTMEG

PINCHES OF GROUND CAYENNE, SALT AND SAFFRON THREADS

1 TBSP OLIVE OIL

60G PARSNIP, PEELED AND DICED

60G SPRING ONIONS, DICED

60G COURGETTE, DICED

2 FREE-RANGE EGGS, PLUS 2 YOLKS

20G SUGAR

80G PLAIN FLOUR

SALT

Put the milk in a pan with the butter and 100g of the diced carrots. Add a grating of nutmeg and generous pinches of cayenne pepper, salt and saffron. Bring to a gentle simmer and cook for 20 minutes until the carrots are done. Tip everything into a blender and blitz until smooth, then set the mixture aside to cool.

Heat the oil in a pan and gently cook the remaining carrots and the rest of the vegetables until tender. Season them with a little salt, then leave to cool. Preheat the oven to 220°C/Fan 200°C/Gas 7.

Whisk the eggs, yolks and sugar together and add a couple of tablespoons of the milk and carrot purée to help loosen the mixture. Add the flour and mix well. Finally, fold in the cooked vegetables and the rest of the milk and carrot purée.

Grease your moulds if necessary – see above. Pour the mixture into the moulds and place them in the oven. For small canelés, cook at 240°C/Fan 220°C/Gas 9 for 10 minutes, then turn the oven down to 160°C/Fan 140°C/Gas 3 for another 20 minutes. For large ones, cook for 15 minutes at 240°C/Fan 220°C/Gas 9 and then 20 minutes at 180°C/Fan 160°C/Gas 4. Turn the cakes out of the moulds and serve warm or cold.

TOPINAMBOURS BOULANGÈRES

Jerusalem Artichoke & Potato Gratin

I like to adapt the classic potato boulangère by adding other root vegetables – in this instance, Jerusalem artichokes. A wholesome and filling dish, this is easy to prepare and will keep in the fridge for a week. Good with chicken and red meat.

Serves 6

1 TBSP VEGETABLE OIL

2 ONIONS, PEELED AND FINELY CHOPPED

2 GARLIC CLOVES, PEELED AND FINELY CHOPPED

2 TBSP BUTTER

500G WAXY POTATOES, PEELED AND SLICED 5MM THICK

800G JERUSALEM ARTICHOKES, PEELED AND SLICED 5MM THICK

4 BAY LEAVES

350ML WHITE CHICKEN STOCK

SALT AND FRESHLY GROUND BLACK PEPPER

Heat the oil in a pan and gently cook the onions and garlic until soft. Preheat the oven to 220°C/Fan 200°C/Gas 7.

Lightly grease an ovenproof dish with some of the butter. Add layer of potatoes and artichoke slices, followed by a couple of bay leaves and half the onions. Season with salt and pepper. Repeat the layers, then pour over the stock. Press the layers down and dot with the remaining butter.

Cover the dish with foil and cook in the preheated oven for 30 minutes. Turn the heat down to 200°C/Fan 180°C/Gas 6, remove the foil and cook for a further 45 minutes.

RIZ ROUGE DE CAMARGUE

Camargue Red Rice

Red rice, grown on the wetlands of the Camargue in southern France, makes a pleasant change from other rice and has an appealing flavour and chewy texture. It lends itself to all cooking styles and is good for salads. This rice is also said to be particularly nutritious.

Serves 4

3 TBSP OLIVE OIL

160G CAMARGUE RED RICE

360ML VEGETABLE STOCK

2 GARLIC CLOVES, FLATTENED WITH A KNIFE

1 ROSEMARY SPRIG

SALT AND FRESHLY GROUND BLACK PEPPER

Heat 2 tablespoons of the oil in an ovenproof pan. Add the rice and cook it for 3–4 minutes over a medium heat, stirring well to coat all the grains with oil. Preheat the oven to 200°C/Fan 180°C/Gas 6.

Add the stock, garlic and rosemary. Cover the pan with a tight-fitting lid and bake the rice in the oven for 60 minutes.

Remove the pan from the oven and set it aside for 10 minutes with the lid on. Then remove the garlic and rosemary, season well and drizzle over the remaining oil. Serve hot or cold.

POMMES DE TERRE ÉCRASÉES
Crushed Potatoes

This is an excellent accompaniment for a roast – it's not just potatoes but packed full of green goodness as well. Serve with a slice of ham and it's a meal.

Serves 4

500G WAXY POTATOES, SUCH AS CHARLOTTES

100G BABY SPINACH LEAVES, WASHED

12 WILD GARLIC LEAVES, IF AVAILABLE, OR 2 GARLIC CLOVES, PEELED AND FINELY CHOPPED

1 TBSP CRÈME FRAÎCHE

2 TBSP OLIVE OIL

2 TBSP SNIPPED CHIVES

2 TBSP CHOPPED PARSLEY

SALT AND FRESHLY GROUND BLACK PEPPER

Wash the potatoes and cook them in a pan of salted water until tender, then drain them and peel off the skins. Put them back in the pan.

Put the spinach in a food processor with the garlic, crème fraîche, olive oil and season with salt and pepper. Blitz until smooth.

Add the spinach mixture to the potatoes and mix with a fork, crushing the potatoes but keeping them fairly chunky. Warm everything through gently, then add the chives and parsley and serve.

LENTILLES À LA MAROCAINE
Lentils Moroccan Style

French cookery has been much influenced by North African cuisine and this is a perfect example. This is a dish that's easy to make and is full of warmth and goodness.

Serves 4

240G BROWN LENTILS

4 TBSP OLIVE OIL

1 MEDIUM ONION, PEELED AND CHOPPED

4 GARLIC CLOVES, PEELED AND CHOPPED

1 TBSP RAS-EL-HANOUT

1 TSP CUMIN SEEDS

4 LARGE TOMATOES, PEELED, SEEDED AND ROUGHLY CHOPPED

ABOUT 350ML VEGETABLE STOCK

2 TBSP FLAKED ALMONDS

1 BUNCH OF CORIANDER, CHOPPED

SALT AND FRESHLY GROUND BLACK PEPPER

Rinse the lentils and check them over for stones, then put them in a large pan and add enough water to cover. Bring to the boil and cook the lentils for 15 minutes, then drain them and set aside.

Rinse and dry the pan, then heat the oil and add the onion and garlic. Cook them gently until tender, stirring often, but don't let them brown.

Add the spices to the pan and continue to cook for 5 minutes, then add the tomatoes and the drained lentils. Season and add enough vegetable stock to come level with the contents of the pan. Cover and simmer for 20 minutes. Meanwhile, toast the almonds in a dry pan.

When the lentils are ready, add the coriander, then tip everything into a serving bowl and top with the toasted flaked almonds.

RIZ À LA BASQUAISE
Rice with Peppers, Basque Style

This is a hearty dish that makes an excellent accompaniment to grilled fish or can be served on its own, hot or cold. Do use a proper Spanish short-grain rice such as Calasparra or Bomba.

Serves 6

3 TBSP OLIVE OIL, PLUS EXTRA
TO SERVE

2 ONIONS, PEELED AND SLICED

3 GARLIC CLOVES, PEELED AND SLICED

6 PLUM TOMATOES, PEELED, SEEDED
AND ROUGHLY CHOPPED

3 RED PEPPERS, SEEDED AND THINLY
SLICED

1 TSP THYME LEAVES

2 TSP SMOKED PAPRIKA

2 TSP PIMENT D'ESPELETTE (SEE PAGE
8), OR CHILLI FLAKES

400G SPANISH SHORT-GRAIN RICE

800ML VEGETABLE STOCK

4 TBSP COARSELY CHOPPED PARSLEY

SALT AND FRESHLY GROUND
BLACK PEPPER

Preheat the oven to 200°C/Fan 180°C/Gas 6. Heat the olive oil in a large ovenproof pan, then add the onions and garlic and cook them gently until soft.

Add the tomatoes and cook for 5 minutes, then add the peppers, thyme, paprika and piment d'espelette or chilli flakes (add more chilli if you like your food spicy), followed by the rice. Continue to cook for another 5 minutes while stirring to coat the rice with the tomatoes and spices.

Pour in the stock, season and bring to the boil. Cover the pan, place it in the oven and cook for 25–30 minutes. Fluff the rice with a fork, then serve garnished with parsley and a little extra oil.

LENTILLES DU PUY

Green Lentils

Considered the best of all lentils, Puy lentils are grown in the region around Le Puy in south-central France. They have a fine flavour and hold their shape well when cooked so they're good for salads as well as soups and other dishes. They are traditionally served with sausages in France but they make a good meal on their own too.

Serves 6

250G GREEN PUY LENTILS

1 TBSP OLIVE OIL

80G SMOKED BACON OR VENTRÉCHE (SEE PAGE 8), DICED

1 CELERY STICK, DICED

1 CARROT, PEELED AND DICED

2 GARLIC CLOVES, CRUSHED

1 ONION, PEELED

2 CLOVES

1 BOUQUET GARNI (SEE PAGE 8)

SALT AND FRESHLY GROUND BLACK PEPPER

To serve (optional)

BUTTER OR OIL

FRENCH DRESSING (SEE PAGE 66)

Rinse the lentils in cold water and check them over for stones. Warm the oil in a pan, add the bacon or ventréche and cook it over a medium heat until just starting to brown. Add the celery, carrot and garlic and cook gently for 5–6 minutes, stirring often.

Stud the onion with the cloves and place it in the pan, then add the bouquet garni and lentils.

Pour in 600ml of water and bring to the boil, then turn the heat down to a gentle simmer. Skim any scum off the surface, then partially cover the pan and leave the lentils to simmer for 30 minutes. They should be tender but still holding their shape.

Remove the onion and bouquet garni, then season with salt and pepper.

If serving the lentils as a vegetable, stir in a little butter or olive oil to taste. If serving as a salad, drain off any excess liquid and dress with a classic French dressing.

FLAGEOLETS AUX OIGNONS NOUVEAUX

Flageolet Beans with New Season Onions

Flageolet are my favourite beans. The canned versions are fine but when cooked from dried, flageolet are something else and they keep well in the fridge for up to 10 days. Serve these beans hot with roast lamb or grilled sausages, blitz them into a soup, or leave them to cool and mix them into a salad. Versatile, delicious and inexpensive.

Serves 4

250G DRIED FLAGEOLET BEANS

1 CARROT, PEELED AND CUT INTO BATONS

1 ONION, PEELED AND STUDDED WITH 2 CLOVES

2 BAY LEAVES

8 NEW SEASON ONIONS WITH GREEN TOPS (OR 12 SPRING ONIONS)

2 TBSP BUTTER

SALT AND FRESHLY GROUND BLACK PEPPER

Soak the beans overnight, then drain them and put them in a large pan with the carrot, clove-studded onion and the bay leaves. Cover with cold water by about 3cm, bring to a simmer and cook for 30 minutes.

Add the white part of the onions, cover and simmer for a further 45 minutes. You may need to top up the pan with some boiling water.

When the beans are tender, take the pan off the heat, add some of the sliced green part of the onions and mix in the butter. Season well and serve.

TARTE À LA TOMATE
Tomato Tart

Delicious any time, this tart is a favourite of mine in the summer months. The richness of the pastry is offset by the light filling and the mustard adds extra flavour. Don't be tempted to leave out the polenta – it soaks up any juices so keeps the pastry crisp.

Serves 6

8–12 TOMATOES (A MIXTURE OF COLOURS IS NICE)

200G PUFF PASTRY

2 TBSP DIJON MUSTARD

1 TBSP POLENTA

1 TBSP THYME LEAVES

ABOUT 1 TBSP GOOD OLIVE OIL

SALT AND FRESHLY GROUND BLACK PEPPER

Slice the tomatoes 5mm thick and lay them out on a rack. Sprinkle a little salt over them and leave them for 20 minutes to render excess water. Pat the slices dry with a clean tea towel or some kitchen paper.

Preheat the oven to 200°C/Fan 180°C/Gas 6. Roll out the puff pastry to fit a 26cm flan ring. Prick the pastry with a fork, then line it with greaseproof paper and fill it with baking beans.

Blind-bake the tart case for 20 minutes. Remove the paper and beans and bake for another 10 minutes. Remove the tart case from the oven. Leave the oven on.

Spread the mustard over the base of the tart, then sprinkle over the polenta. Arrange the tomato slices in the tart, then season with a little pepper and the thyme leaves.

Drizzle the olive oil over the tomatoes and bake the tart for 20 minutes. Serve hot, warm or cold.

TARTES FINES AUX PETIT POIS
Pea & Mint Tarts

Light and delicious, brik pastry is Tunisian in origin, but has become a staple ingredient in France. It is similar to filo but more robust and easier to work with. Using brik instead of shortcrust or puff in these tarts makes them lighter and less calorific than the traditional versions.

Serves 6

OLIVE OIL

12 SHEETS OF BRIK PASTRY

320G PEAS (FROZEN ARE FINE)

1 GARLIC CLOVE, PEELED

ZEST AND JUICE OF 1 LEMON

2 TBSP CRÈME FRAÎCHE

2 SPRING ONIONS, SLICED

BUNCH OF MINT, CHOPPED

SALT AND FRESHLY GROUND BLACK PEPPER

Brush 4 tartlet tins, 8cm in diameter, with a little olive oil. Preheat the oven to 200°C/Fan 180°C/Gas 6.

Cut out 12 circles of brik pastry measuring about 10cm in diameter – you can use a side plate as a template. Layer 3 sheets into each tin, brushing each layer with a little olive oil. Add some baking paper and baking beans to each tin to weigh the pastry down. Bake the pastry cases for 20 minutes until they are crisp and browned. Leave them to cool, then take them out of the tins.

Bring a pan of salted water to the boil, add the peas and the garlic and bring the water back to the boil. (If you are using fresh peas, you might need to cook them for a little longer until they're tender.) Drain and refresh the peas in a bowl of iced water, then drain them again.

Put half the peas with the garlic in a blender and add the lemon zest, crème fraîche and 4 tablespoons of water. Season with salt and pepper, then blitz until smooth. Spoon the mixture into the tart cases.

Dress the remaining peas with the lemon juice, sliced spring onions, mint and a tablespoon of olive oil and season. Divide the peas between the tarts, then serve.

REPAS DE FAMILLE

Family Meals

French food doesn't have to be time-consuming and take all day to prepare. In this chapter you will find plenty of recipes that are quick to make and others that can be prepped in advance and left to cook. I do think that coming together to enjoy a good meal — even if it's only for 20 minutes — is a vital part of family life.

NOUILLES AUX CREVETTES ET PISTOU

Pasta with Prawns & Pistou

People are often surprised to learn that pasta is a staple in France, eaten on an almost daily basis. Dried egg pasta, such as tagliatelle or fettuccine, is perfect for this recipe, but any shape will do.

Serves 4

16 CHERRY TOMATOES

OLIVE OIL

320G DRIED EGG PASTA

160G COOKED PEELED PRAWNS (ABOUT 12 LARGE PRAWNS)

6 TBSP PISTOU (SEE PAGE 288)

SALT AND FRESHLY GROUND BLACK PEPPER

Preheat the oven to 200°C/Fan 180°C/Gas 6. Cut the tomatoes in half and put them in a roasting tin. Season them with salt and pepper and drizzle with a little olive oil, then cook them in the oven for 20 minutes.

Boil the pasta in plenty of salted water until cooked.

Drain the pasta, then tip it back into the pan. Add the prawns and roasted tomatoes, then stir in the pistou and serve at once.

NOUILLES AUX POIVRONS ET TAPENADE
Pasta with Peppers & Tapenade

As I've said, the French love their pasta and this simple dish makes a perfect one-pot supper. You can, of course, roast and peel the peppers yourself, but for speed use a jar of piquillo peppers – they're sweet, smoky and very convenient. Tapenade is a great thing to have in your store-cupboard but again, you can make it yourself if you prefer.

Serves 4

360G DRIED EGG PASTA

120G PIQUILLO PEPPERS, SLICED

2 TBSP TAPENADE (SEE PAGE 30 OR SHOP-BOUGHT)

OLIVE OIL

BASIL LEAVES

SALT AND FRESHLY GROUND BLACK PEPPER

Bring a large pan of salted water to the boil and cook the pasta according to the packet instructions.

Once the pasta is cooked, drain it but do not rinse, then tip it back into the pan. Stir in the sliced peppers, tapenade and a little drizzle of oil, then check the seasoning. Finish with some basil and serve at once.

NOUILLES AUX TRÉSORS DES BOIS
Pasta with Wild Mushrooms

A celebration of wild mushrooms in a bowl, this is a really quick meal. If you can't get wild mushrooms, use a mix of cultivated such as shiitake, oyster or shimeji.

Serves 4

2 TBSP VEGETABLE OIL

400G MIXED MUSHROOMS, CLEANED AND TRIMMED

1 SHALLOT, PEELED AND FINELY CHOPPED

2 GARLIC CLOVES, PEELED AND FINELY CHOPPED

1 TSP THYME LEAVES

2 TBSP BRANDY

4 TBSP CRÈME FRAÎCHE

300G DRIED EGG PASTA, SUCH AS TAGLIATELLE

SALT AND FRESHLY GROUND BLACK PEPPER

Heat the oil in a pan and fry the mushrooms until they have taken on a little colour. Add the shallot, garlic and thyme, then season with salt and pepper and take the pan off the heat.

Pick out about a third of the best-looking mushrooms and set them aside. Put the rest of the mushrooms in a blender, add the brandy and crème fraîche, then blend until smooth.

Meanwhile, bring a pan of salted water to the boil and cook the pasta according to the packet instructions.

Drain the pasta, but do not rinse it, then tip it back in the pan. Stir in the mushroom purée and check the seasoning. Serve at once, topped with the reserved whole mushrooms.

TAGLIATELLE, SAUCE SARDINE PIMENTÉE

Pasta with Sardine & Chilli Sauce

Every French household has dried pasta and cans of fish in the store-cupboard for making speedy, tasty suppers like this one. It's not haute cuisine but is none the worse for that.

Serves 2

180G DRIED TAGLIATELLE

2 TBSP EXTRA VIRGIN OLIVE OIL

1 SHALLOT, CHOPPED

1 GARLIC CLOVE, CHOPPED

1 FRESH RED CHILLI, CHOPPED

125G CAN OF SARDINES IN OIL

BASIL OR GRATED PARMESAN CHEESE

SALT AND FRESHLY GROUND
BLACK PEPPER

Cook the pasta in plenty of boiling, salted water according to the instructions on the packet. Drain, reserving a couple of spoonfuls of the cooking water.

Meanwhile, heat the oil in a large pan and sweat the shallot, garlic and chilli for a few minutes until softened. Add the sardines (with their oil) and crush them with a fork.

Add the drained pasta to the pan, along with the spoonfuls of cooking water, then toss until mixed well and emulsified. Season to taste and serve sprinkled with a little basil or grated Parmesan.

GÂTEAU DE POMME DE TERRE AU JAMBON DE PAYS

Ham & Potato Cake

A hearty, rustic dish, this can be served on its own, with some vegetables, or you can make individual servings in little tartlet tins. In France, I would use Bayonne ham, but Parma or Serrano are also fine.

Serves 4

1KG FLOURY POTATOES (SUCH AS KING EDWARDS OR ROOSTERS), PEELED

2 TBSP BUTTER, PLUS EXTRA FOR GREASING

1 SHALLOT, PEELED AND CHOPPED

4 FREE-RANGE EGG YOLKS

GRATING OF NUTMEG

1 BUNCH OF CHIVES

8 THIN SLICES OF AIR-DRIED HAM, SUCH AS BAYONNE (SEE PAGE 8), PARMA OR SERRANO

SALT AND FRESHLY GROUND BLACK PEPPER

Cut the potatoes in half (or into quarters if large) and boil them in salted water until just cooked. Pass them through a ricer into a bowl.

Heat the butter in a pan and gently cook the shallot. Add it to the potato with the egg yolks, nutmeg, chives and seasoning, then mix well.

Preheat the oven to 180°C/Fan 160°C/Gas 4. Butter a 28cm flan dish and spoon in the mixture, then roll up the ham slices and place them on top. They don't need to be too neat but push them in a little so they stay put.

Bake for 40 minutes, then leave to cool down a little before serving.

QUICHE AUX POIREAUX ET SAUMON

Leek & Salmon Quiche

This is a lighter, healthier variation on the traditional quiche Lorraine. I have cut back on the cream but there are dishes that just have to contain some — and this is one of them. Serve this freshly cooked and warm but never cold from the fridge, as all the delicate flavours would be lost. You will need a tart ring measuring about 26cm in diameter and 4cm in height.

Serves 6–8

1 TBSP BUTTER, PLUS EXTRA FOR GREASING

200G SHORTCRUST PASTRY (SEE PAGE 294)

1 EGG, BEATEN (FOR EGG WASH)

1 LARGE LEEK (WHITE PART ONLY)

200G HOT-SMOKED SALMON, FLAKED

2 FREE-RANGE EGGS, PLUS 6 YOLKS

100ML DOUBLE CREAM

400ML MILK

1 PINCH OF FRESHLY GROUND NUTMEG

100G GRUYÈRE CHEESE, GRATED (OPTIONAL)

SALT AND FRESHLY GROUND BLACK PEPPER

Preheat the oven to 200°C/Fan 180°C/Gas 6. Butter the tart ring. Roll the pastry out to a thickness of 3mm and use it to line the tart ring, making sure it is well pressed into the edges. Trim off any excess pastry.

Prick the base with a fork, then line it with greaseproof paper and fill it with baking beans. Bake the pastry for 15 minutes, then remove the beans and paper. Brush the inside with beaten egg and cook for a further 10 minutes. Remove the tart case from the oven and leave it to cool. Leave the oven on.

Cut the white part of the leek in half lengthways, then across into thin slices. Wash the slices well. Melt the butter in a pan, add the leek slices and cook them gently for 20 minutes until tender. Season, then add the leek to the pastry case, followed by the salmon.

Whisk the eggs, yolks, cream and milk together in a jug and season with salt, pepper and nutmeg. Pull the oven shelf halfway out and place the tin on the shelf. Slowly pour the egg mixture into the pastry case and sprinkle over the cheese, if using. Gently push the shelf back in.

Bake the quiche for 10 minutes, then turn the heat down to 180°C/Fan 160°C/Gas 4 and cook for a further 20 minutes. The quiche should have risen a little, have a slight wobble to it and a lovely golden colour. Leave it to cool slightly before slicing.

PAVÉ DE THON ANTIBOISE
Tuna Steaks Antiboise

Light, quick and simple, this recipe is great with tuna, but other oily fish such as salmon and sardines also work well, as does red mullet. Antiboise sauce originated in the French city of Antibes and is a variation on sauce vierge, using the flavours of Provence.

Serves 4

2 LEMONS

4 TBSP OLIVE OIL

4 X 120−160G TUNA STEAKS

1 TBSP PINE NUTS

2 MEDIUM RED TOMATOES, PEELED, SEEDED AND DICED

1 GARLIC CLOVE, PEELED AND CHOPPED

2 TBSP DICED PITTED BLACK OLIVES

1 TBSP CAPERS IN VINEGAR, DRAINED

1 SHALLOT, PEELED AND FINELY CHOPPED

HANDFUL OF BASIL LEAVES, TORN

SALT AND FRESHLY GROUND BLACK PEPPER

Peel the lemons, removing all the white pith, and divide them into segments. Do this over a bowl so you collect any juice.

Rub a little oil over the steaks and season them with salt and pepper. Place a pan over a high heat and when it's hot, add the tuna steaks. Sear them until they're nicely browned − 2 minutes should be enough, depending on the thickness of the steaks − then flip them over and cook them for a further 2 minutes. Take the steaks out of the pan and keep them warm.

Toast the pine nuts in a dry pan, then add the tomatoes, lemon segments and juice, garlic, olives, capers, shallot and 2 tablespoons of water and warm everything through. Add the torn basil leaves and serve the sauce warm with the tuna.

CALAMAR BRAISÉ AU VIN ROUGE
Braised Squid in Red Wine

This is a hearty dish that has bags of flavour, but is low in fat, and never fails to impress. Squid should be cooked briefly over a high heat, or for a long time over a low heat until tender, as in this recipe. Serve with boiled potatoes or some Camargue red rice (see page 124) to soak up the delicious sauce. Ask your fishmonger to clean the squid for you.

Serves 4-6

800G CLEANED SQUID

2 TBSP OLIVE OIL

2 ONIONS, PEELED AND SLICED

2 GARLIC CLOVES, PEELED AND CHOPPED

500ML FULL-BODIED RED WINE

3 STAR ANISE, 2 CLOVES, 1 TSP BLACK PEPPERCORNS, TIED UP IN A PIECE OF MUSLIN

2 TBSP SQUID INK

250ML GOOD-QUALITY TOMATO JUICE

250ML CHICKEN STOCK

2 TBSP CHOPPED PARSLEY

SALT AND FRESHLY GROUND BLACK PEPPER

If the squid is large, cut the body into rings. Small ones can be left whole, but separate the tentacles.

Preheat the oven to 180°C/Fan 160°C/Gas 4. Heat the oil in a lidded ovenproof pan or a flameproof casserole dish and cook the sliced onions and garlic over a medium heat until they are starting to colour. Add the squid and cook for 5 minutes, then add half the wine and continue to cook until the pan is almost dry.

Add the remaining wine and the bag of spices, then season with salt and pepper and continue to simmer for 10 minutes. Add the squid ink, tomato juice and stock.

Cover the pan, place it in the oven and cook the squid for 1 hour or until tender. Add the parsley and serve.

MOULES À LA BIÈRE

Mussels with Beer

Mussels are cheap, good to eat and make a great one-pot dish. I like to cook them in beer which gives a fuller flavour and is less acidic than wine. If you like a little sharpness, add a squeeze of lemon at the end. Serve with thick slices of grilled sourdough baguette, maybe rubbed with a little garlic. If you are feeling up to it, pick all the mussels from the shells and gently reheat them in the sauce. Otherwise, I'm happy with the rustic, informal version — as they say in French 'à la bonne franquette'.

Serves 4

1.6KG MUSSELS

340ML BEER (LIGHT LAGER OR WHEAT OR FRUIT BEER)

2 SHALLOTS, PEELED AND FINELY CHOPPED

2 GARLIC CLOVES, PEELED AND FINELY CHOPPED

2 TSP CRACKED BLACK PEPPER

4 TBSP CRÈME FRAÎCHE

Wash the mussels and scrape off the beards and any barnacles. Discard any mussels that don't close when they're tapped.

Heat a large pan until very hot, then add the beer, shallots, garlic and cracked pepper, followed by the mussels. Cover the pan with a tight-fitting lid, then give the mussels a stir after 2 minutes.

The mussels should take 6–7 minutes to cook. Drain them, reserving the liquid. Discard any mussels that don't open.

Tip the cooking liquor back into the pan and bring it to the boil, then add the crème fraîche and simmer for a further 5 minutes. Add the mussels, then serve.

FILETS DE MAQUEREAUX À LA MOUTARDE

Grilled Mackerel Fillets with Mustard

Mackerel is cheap compared to many kinds of fish and makes an excellent quick meal. No oil is needed here, as the fish is naturally oily, and the mustard provides the seasoning so you don't have to add any salt either. The sharpness of the mustard works perfectly with the fish and I like to serve this with grilled asparagus and boiled new potatoes.

Serves 4

4 FILLETS OF MACKEREL, PIN-BONED

2 TBSP DIJON MUSTARD

Take the fillets and carefully cut 5 or 6 slits, about 5mm deep, in the skin side of each one.

Brush the mustard evenly over the skin of the fillets. Preheat your grill.

Place the fillets, skin-side up, under the hot grill. The skin should blister and start to burn and the fish should take no more than 5 minutes to cook through. Serve the fish at once.

DAURADE ROYALE EN CROÛTE DE SEL
Gilthead Bream Cooked in a Salt Crust

From the northern coast of Brittany all the way round to the Italian border, this way of cooking fish is the first choice for lovers of simplicity and pure flavour. It's so healthy too, as no fat is needed, although I do like to serve this with a dressing of herbs, olive oil and orange juice. This recipe works with most fish but for me, a wild bream is best.

Serves 2

1 X 600−800G GILTHEAD BREAM (OR COD, LING, HAKE, POLLOCK OR BASS)

1KG COARSE SEA SALT

2 TBSP PLAIN FLOUR

1 TBSP CRACKED BLACK PEPPER

2 EGG WHITES

2 BAY LEAVES, CHOPPED

1 TBSP CHOPPED THYME

1 TBSP CRUSHED FENNEL SEEDS

Herb & Orange Dressing

200ML OLIVE OIL

JUICE OF 1 ORANGE AND ZEST OF ½

1 TBSP CHOPPED PARSLEY

1 TBSP CHOPPED CHIVES

1 TBSP CHOPPED DILL OR FENNEL TOPS

HANDFUL OF BASIL

SALT AND FRESHLY GROUND BLACK PEPPER

Gut the fish, if this has not already been done by your fishmonger, and snip off the fins but do not scale it.

Mix the salt with the flour, pepper, egg whites, herbs and fennel seeds. Preheat the oven to 240°C/Fan 220°C/Gas 9.

Sprinkle a third of the salt mix on the bottom of a cast-iron dish or a roasting tin. Lay the fish on top, then cover it with the remaining salt and pat it down. The fish should be completely covered.

Cook the fish in the oven for 15 minutes, then remove it and leave it to rest for 3−4 minutes.

To make the dressing, put the oil, juice, zest and herbs in a blender and blitz for 30 seconds. Season with salt and pepper. This dressing can be kept in the fridge for up to 5 days, but it will lose its green colour.

Carefully break the salt crust and remove the skin from the fish. Serve the fish with the dressing.

TOMATES FARCIES À L'ANCIENNE
Stuffed Tomatoes

This is a good, economical family dish served in French households up and down the land. My mother used to cook it, so did my grandmother and so do I. It's best made in the summer when tomatoes are at their best and cheapest. Although this is traditionally accompanied by rice to soak up the juices, you could just serve it with a salad for a lighter meal.

Serves 8

8 LARGE BEEF TOMATOES

4 GARLIC CLOVES, PEELED AND VERY FINELY CHOPPED

2 ONIONS, PEELED AND VERY FINELY CHOPPED

100G BREADCRUMBS

1 FREE-RANGE EGG, BEATEN

4 TBSP CHOPPED PARSLEY

600G MINCED BEEF

200G MINCED PORK

OLIVE OIL

SALT AND FRESHLY GROUND BLACK PEPPER

Take the tomatoes and cut a slice, about 5mm thick, from the top of each one. Set these lids aside. Carefully remove all the seeds and water from the inside. Sprinkle a little salt inside the tomatoes, turn them upside down and leave them to drain for 20 minutes. Preheat the oven to 200°C/Fan 180°C/Gas 6.

Mix the garlic and onions with the breadcrumbs, egg and parsley. Season the mixture well and then work in the meats until well mixed. Stuff the tomatoes with the filling and put the lids on top. Place the tomatoes in a roasting tin and drizzle them with olive oil. Bake them in the preheated oven for 40 minutes.

Serve with rice or bread to soak up all the juices or just with a salad.

POULET RÔTI AUX HERBES
Roast Chicken with Herbs

A good roast chicken is always a favourite meal and this is a particularly delicious version. A herby stuffing is added under the skin to keep the meat moist while imparting lots of flavour. The stuffing is light, made with fromage blanc and very little butter. A root vegetable gratin (see page 123) is a good accompaniment for this.

Serves 4–6

JUICE AND ZEST OF 1 LEMON

1 TBSP BUTTER

3 TBSP FROMAGE BLANC (LIGHT CREAM CHEESE)

1 TBSP CHOPPED CHIVES

1 TBSP CHOPPED PARSLEY

1 HANDFUL OF ROCKET

1 TSP THYME LEAVES

2 TBSP BREADCRUMBS

OLIVE OIL

1 X 1.6KG CHICKEN

100ML WHITE WINE

1 TSP TOMATO PASTE

120ML CHICKEN STOCK

SALT AND FRESHLY GROUND BLACK PEPPER

Preheat the oven to 240°C/Fan 220°C/Gas 9. Put the lemon juice and zest, butter, fromage blanc, chives, parsley, rocket, thyme and breadcrumbs in a blender or food processor. Season with salt and pepper, then blitz to make a smooth paste.

Lightly oil your fingers. Carefully lift the skin away from the breast and legs of the chicken, then slide your fingers under the skin to loosen it. Fill a piping bag with the stuffing and squeeze this under the skin in an even layer.

You will have some stuffing left, so put this in the cavity of the chicken. Rub the chicken with olive oil and season it, then put it in a roasting tin. Roast the chicken for 20 minutes at the high temperature, then reduce the heat to 200°C/Fan 180°C/Gas 6 and cook for another 30 minutes. Check that the chicken is done by piercing the thickest part of the leg with a skewer – the juices should run clear.

Transfer the chicken to a plate or board, tipping any juices from the cavity into the roasting tin. Cover the chicken with foil and leave it to rest for 20 minutes.

Place the roasting tin on the hob and simmer the cooking juices. Add the wine and tomato paste, then simmer until the liquid is reduced by half. Add the stock and reduce again until the sauce is syrupy. Serve with the chicken.

POULET BASQUAISE
Basque—Style Chicken

This is a really good simple supper — everything you need in one pot. I like to make it with chicken legs, as they are more flavourful than breast and less likely to be dry. Espelette chillies are grown in the Basque region in southwest France and have a beautifully mild, fragrant taste that is perfect for this dish. If you can't find any, just use other chillies to taste. This is a dish that's even better when made in advance and then reheated.

Serves 4

12 NEW POTATOES, SCRUBBED

4 CHICKEN LEGS

1 TBSP SMOKED PAPRIKA

4 TBSP OLIVE OIL

2 RED, GREEN OR YELLOW PEPPERS, HALVED AND SEEDED

2 ONIONS, PEELED AND THINLY SLICED

6 GARLIC CLOVES, PEELED AND CHOPPED

3 BAY LEAVES

2 THYME SPRIGS

200ML WHITE WINE

1 TBSP PIMENT D'ESPELETTE (SEE PAGE 8) OR CHILLI FLAKES

4 LARGE TOMATOES, PEELED AND DICED

SALT AND FRESHLY GROUND BLACK PEPPER

Cut the potatoes in half, put them in a pan of salted water and bring to the boil. Cook them for 10 minutes, then drain and set aside.

Joint the chicken legs into thighs and drumsticks — or ask your butcher to do this for you. Season them with salt and smoked paprika. Heat the oil in an ovenproof pan or a flameproof casserole dish and fry the chicken pieces until golden brown on both sides. Remove them from the pan and set them aside.

Slice the peppers into long strips and fry them in the same pan until tender, then add the onions, garlic and par-boiled potatoes. Cook them over a medium heat for 5–6 minutes. Preheat the oven to 200°C/Fan 180°C/Gas 6.

Tie the bay leaves and thyme sprigs together and add them to the pan along with the wine and piment d'espelette or chilli flakes. Add extra chilli if you like your food really spicy.

Add the tomatoes, then put the chicken and any juices back into the pan and stir gently. Put a lid on the pan or cover it tightly with foil and place it in the oven for 30 minutes or until the chicken juices run clear. Check the seasoning, then serve or set aside to enjoy later.

LAPIN RÔTI AU THYM

Roast Rabbit with Thyme

Rustic family fare, this is the easiest dish to prepare and produces beautiful golden-brown nuggets of meat. Just bring it all to the table and let everyone chew on the bones – very French 'finger food'! Good served with Tomates à la Provençale (see page 112).

Serves 4

1 WHOLE RABBIT

2 TBSP THYME LEAVES

4–6 TBSP OLIVE OIL

12 SMALL ONIONS OR SHALLOTS, PEELED

16 GARLIC CLOVES, PEELED

SALT AND FRESHLY GROUND BLACK PEPPER

Ask your butcher to joint the rabbit, cutting the legs into 2 pieces, the saddle into 3 and the shoulders and front into 2. Preheat the oven to 220°C/Fan 200°C/Gas 7.

Put the rabbit in a large roasting tin and season with salt and pepper and a tablespoon of the thyme leaves. Add the oil and toss until the rabbit is well coated. Place the tin in the oven and roast for 20 minutes.

Add the onions or shallots and the garlic, then stir well and roast for another 15 minutes, stirring again halfway through. Add the remaining thyme before serving.

SUPRÊMES DE VOLAILLE À LA DIABLE
Devilled Chicken Breasts

The traditional version of this is deep-fried, but I prefer to bake the chicken breasts for a lighter result. I serve this with a peppery watercress salad for a quick and easy meal.

Serves 4

1 TBSP DIJON MUSTARD

1 TSP CAYENNE PEPPER, OR MORE TO TASTE

4 SKINLESS CHICKEN BREASTS

1 FREE-RANGE EGG

60G BREADCRUMBS

OLIVE OIL

SALT

Watercress Salad

240G WATERCRESS, WASHED

1 SHALLOT, PEELED AND SLICED

JUICE OF 1 LEMON

3 TBSP EXTRA VIRGIN OLIVE OIL

SALT AND FRESHLY GROUND BLACK PEPPER

Mix the mustard with the cayenne and spread the mixture all over the chicken breasts, then leave them to marinate in the fridge for an hour. Preheat the oven to 210°C /Fan 190°C/Gas 6½.

Beat the egg in a shallow bowl and season it with a little salt. Spread the breadcrumbs on a plate. Dip each chicken breast in the egg, then into the breadcrumbs, pressing it down so the crumbs stick to the meat.

Place the coated breasts on an oiled baking tray, then drizzle a little oil over them. Bake them in the oven for 15 minutes, then leave to rest for 5 minutes.

For the salad, put the watercress in a bowl, then mix the remaining ingredients together to make the dressing. Dress the salad and serve it with the chicken breasts.

CÔTE DE PORC AUX PRUNEAUX
Pork Chops with Prunes

Prunes go well with pork and this is a quick dish to make. When you're buying chops, ask for those from nearer the neck, which tend to be more marbled with fat so not dry. Some cooks like to add cream to the sauce, but I think it's lighter and fresher without.

Serves 4

100G PITTED PRUNES

1 TSP CASTER SUGAR

½ CINNAMON STICK

1 STAR ANISE

200ML RED WINE

1 TBSP VEGETABLE OIL

4 PORK CHOPS

2 TBSP BRANDY

125ML BROWN CHICKEN STOCK

SALT AND FRESHLY GROUND
BLACK PEPPER

Place the prunes in a pan with the sugar, spices and red wine. Simmer them for 10 minutes, then remove the pan from the heat, cover it and set it aside to cool.

Preheat the oven to 200°C/Fan 180°C/Gas 6. Heat the oil in an ovenproof pan, season the chops and cook them over a high heat until brown on both sides. Place them in the oven for 10 minutes or until cooked through, depending on the thickness of the chops. Remove them and leave them to rest in a warm place.

To make the sauce, pour the brandy into the pan and add 200ml of the liquid from the prunes. Boil until reduced by half, then add the stock and continue to simmer until you have a syrupy sauce.

Reheat the prunes in the remaining wine and spices and serve the chops with the sauce and prunes.

PAUPIETTES DE BOEUF
Beef Olives

A cheap and filling French classic, paupiettes are similar to a British dish known as beef olives and are a good way of making a piece of meat go a little further. My version is made with beef, but you can also use veal or lamb. If you do use lamb, choose a merguez sausage. Most good butchers should be able to supply caul fat.

Serves 4

1 PIECE OF RUMP OR SIRLOIN
(ABOUT 320G)

240G SAUSAGE MEAT

120G CAUL FAT

OLIVE OIL

1 ONION, SLICED

12 CHESTNUT MUSHROOMS, SLICED

125ML MADEIRA

6 SAGE LEAVES

300ML BEEF OR VEAL STOCK

SALT AND FRESHLY GROUND
BLACK PEPPER

Cutting against the grain of the meat, cut the beef into 4 even slices. Place each slice between 2 sheets of cling film and, using a rolling pin, flatten it out to a thickness of about 3mm.

Divide the sausage meat between the slices and roll each one up. Wrap each one in a piece of caul, then secure with butchers' string.

Heat a little oil in a pan and sear the paupiettes until brown, then remove them and set aside. Add the onion to the pan and cook until browned, then add the mushrooms. Cook them for 5 minutes then pour in the Madeira. When that has evaporated, add the sage and the stock.

Lightly season the stock and put the paupiettes back in the pan. Bring to a gentle simmer, cover loosely with foil and cook for 15 minutes. Take out the paupiettes and boil the sauce rapidly until syrupy. Serve the paupiettes with the sauce. A root vegetable boulangère (see page 123) is a good accompaniment.

STEAK HACHÉ À CHEVAL
Beef Patties Topped with Eggs

Contrary to popular belief, this excellent dish is not made of horsemeat. The term 'à cheval' means on horseback, and indicates that the patties are served with a fried egg on top. Fresh beef patties are sold in most butchers in France, but you can make them yourself very easily. If making your own mince at home, use rump. I like to include a little fat in my patties, but you can go as lean as you like. This makes a great speedy supper served with a green salad and some sautéed potatoes (see page 116).

Serves 4

2 TBSP VEGETABLE OIL

1 LARGE ONION, PEELED AND SLICED

1 TSP SUGAR

2 TSP RED WINE VINEGAR

650G MINCED BEEF

1 TBSP BUTTER

4 FREE-RANGE EGGS

SALT AND FRESHLY GROUND BLACK PEPPER

Heat a tablespoon of the oil in a pan, add the onion and sugar and season with salt and pepper. Cook the onion over a medium heat until it's nicely caramelised, then stir in the vinegar. Remove the onion from the pan and set it aside.

Season the beef and shape it into 4 neat patties. Heat the remaining oil in the pan. Sear the patties on both sides to brown them well, then continue to cook for 6–8 minutes for pink meat.

Heat the butter in a separate frying pan and crack in the eggs. Cover the pan with a lid or some foil to create a little steam and cook the eggs gently until the whites are set but the yolks are still runny.

Serve the patties topped with some caramelised onion and a fried egg.

CHOU-FLEUR ET JAMBON AU GRATIN
Ham & Cauliflower Cheese

An excellent supper dish, this can be prepared well in advance and then finished off in the oven when you're nearly ready to eat.

Serves 6

1 CAULIFLOWER, SPLIT INTO FLORETS

60G BUTTER

60G PLAIN FLOUR

1 LITRE MILK

GRATING OF NUTMEG

6 SLICES OF HAM

120G CHEESE (SUCH AS COMTE OR GRUYÈRE), GRATED

SALT AND FRESHLY GROUND BLACK PEPPER

Bring a pan of water to the boil, add the cauliflower florets and cook for 10 minutes, then drain them well.

Melt the butter in a pan, then stir in the flour and cook over a very low heat for 5 minutes, Don't allow the mixture to brown. Whisk in the milk, turn up the heat and bring the sauce to the boil. Season well with a grating of nutmeg and some salt and pepper, then set the pan aside. Preheat the oven to 200°C/Fan 180°C/Gas 6.

Cut the ham into thin strips. Layer the cauliflower and ham in an ovenproof dish, then pour over the white sauce and sprinkle the cheese on top. Bake in the oven for 15 minutes, then pop the dish under the grill to brown the top more if you like. Serve with salad.

FESTINS GOURMANDS

GOURMANDS

Weekend Treats

The dishes in this chapter are slightly more elaborate than the family meals but they're still not the rich French cuisine of the old days. These are recipes for weekends, when you may have time to spend longer in the kitchen and you're able to linger over a special meal and perhaps a glass or two of wine.

TARTELETTES DE CREVETTES THERMIDOR
Shrimp Tartlets Thermidor

Lobster thermidor is one of the great French classics, but it is expensive and a fiddle to make. My version is lighter and cheaper, using shrimp or prawns and no flour in the sauce, but it still has great flavour. You need 4 tartlet tins, 11cm in diameter and 2cm deep.

Serves 6

180G SHORTCRUST PASTRY (SEE PAGE 294)

½ TBSP BUTTER

1 SHALLOT, PEELED AND VERY FINELY CHOPPED

80ML DRY WHITE WINE

80ML FISH STOCK

½ TBSP DIJON MUSTARD

2 FREE-RANGE EGG YOLKS

100ML WHIPPING CREAM

2 TBSP GRATED PARMESAN CHEESE

1 TBSP TARRAGON LEAVES

120G COOKED PEELED SHRIMP OR SMALL PRAWNS

SALT AND FRESHLY GROUND BLACK PEPPER

Preheat the oven to 200°C/Fan 180°C/Gas 6. Roll out the pastry and use it to line the tins. Prick the pastry with a fork, then cover with greaseproof paper and fill with baking beans.

Blind-bake the tartlet cases for 20 minutes until the pastry is light brown and cooked through. Remove them from the oven and take out the paper and beans.

Melt the butter in a pan and gently cook the shallot until soft. Add the wine and boil until it has reduced by half, then add the stock and reduce again by half. Take the pan off the heat and leave to cool slightly, then mix in the mustard and egg yolks. Leave to cool for another 5 minutes.

Whisk the whipping cream until it forms peaks, then fold it into the cooled sauce with the grated Parmesan and the tarragon.

Turn the oven up to 220°C/Fan 200°C/Gas 7. Divide the shrimp or prawns between the tartlets, then pour in the sauce. Bake the tartlets in the oven for 10 minutes. Serve at once.

GIGOT DE LOTTE PIQUÉ À L'AIL ET ROMARIN

Monkfish Cooked in the Style of Lamb

This is an impressive dish but very easy and quick to cook. You do need a nice chunky piece of monkfish, though, for the recipe to work properly, so talk to your fishmonger. The sauce is full of flavour but not rich – I've kept the amount of cream down and there's not a lot of oil. Lovely served with sautéed new potatoes (see page 116).

Serves 4

4 LARGE GARLIC CLOVES, PEELED

1 LARGE MONKFISH TAIL (ABOUT 1.25KG), BONE IN, SKINNED AND TRIMMED

1 ROSEMARY SPRIG

2 TBSP OLIVE OIL

1 LARGE SHALLOT, PEELED AND CHOPPED

150ML DRY WHITE WINE

4 TBSP CRÈME FRAÎCHE

SALT AND FRESHLY GROUND BLACK PEPPER

Cut each clove of garlic into 4 slices. Cut little incisions in the fish and push a sliver of garlic and a few rosemary needles into each one. Preheat the oven to 220°C/Fan 200°C/Gas 7.

Rub the fish with olive oil and season it well. Heat a tablespoon of oil in a roasting tin on the hob, add the fish and sear it on all sides. Place the tin in the preheated oven and roast the fish for 15 minutes. Remove and take the fish out of the tin, then set it aside to rest in a warm place for 10 minutes.

While the fish is resting, make the sauce. Place the roasting tin over a high heat, add the shallot and cook until it's just starting to colour. Add the wine and any juices that have run from the resting fish and boil for 2–3 minutes. Add the crème fraîche, then bring the sauce back to the boil and check the seasoning.

Take the fish to the table to carve into portions and serve it with the sauce.

MERLANS EN COLÈRE

Angry Whiting

I think deep-fried whiting is a real treat and the tomato compote is lighter than the tartare sauce usually served with it. The whiting are 'angry' because they are chasing their tails! Ask the fishmonger to scale the fish and remove the gills.

Serves 4

4 WHITING (ABOUT 250G EACH), SCALED AND GILLS REMOVED

500ML MILK

BUNCH OF CURLY PARSLEY

PLAIN FLOUR

VEGETABLE OIL, FOR DEEP-FRYING

SALT AND FRESHLY GROUND BLACK PEPPER

Tomato Compote

1 TBSP VEGETABLE OIL

2 SHALLOTS, PEELED AND FINELY CHOPPED

1 GARLIC CLOVE, PEELED AND FINELY CHOPPED

1 RED CHILLI, SLICED

8 PLUM TOMATOES, PEELED, SEEDED AND CHOPPED

JUICE OF 1 LEMON

SALT

For the tomato compote, heat the oil in a pan and sweat the shallots and garlic until softened. Add the sliced chilli, and cook for a further 5 minutes. Add the tomatoes to the pan, season with salt and simmer for 10 minutes, then add the lemon juice and set the compote aside.

Rinse the fish under the cold tap, then put them in a bowl with the milk and leave them to soak for 20 minutes. Wash the parsley and dry it really well.

Drain the whiting, then pat them dry with a cloth or kitchen paper. Season with salt and pepper, then dust the fish in flour. Bend each fish round so that its tail fits into its mouth. Press down firmly – you may need to secure the fish with a wooden stick.

Half fill a large pan or a deep-fat fryer with oil and heat to 180°C. Add 2 of the fish and fry them for 8–10 minutes, until golden and crisp, then set them aside on some kitchen paper to drain while you fry the rest.

Deep-fry the parsley for 30 seconds to crisp it up, then drain and season. Be careful as it will spit. Serve the fish with the fried parsley and the compote.

PASTILLA DE ROUGET
Red Mullet Pastilla

Pastilla is usually made with pigeon and deep-fried, but this baked version with red mullet is lighter and makes a lovely starter. Brik pastry is from North Africa and is similar to filo.

Serves 4

4 FILLETS OF RED MULLET, PIN-BONED

8 SHEETS OF BRIK PASTRY

2 TBSP TAPENADE (SHOP-BOUGHT OR SEE PAGE 30)

16 BASIL LEAVES

1 TBSP PLAIN FLOUR

2 TBSP OLIVE OIL

AÏOLI (SEE PAGE 32), TO SERVE

FRESHLY GROUND BLACK PEPPER

Cut each mullet fillet into 4 long pieces. Season with a little pepper but no salt, as the tapenade is already quite salty. Preheat the oven to 220°C/Fan 200°C/Gas 7.

Cut the brik sheets in half and place a piece of fish in the centre of each half, then top with a little tapenade and basil leaf.

Mix the flour with 2 tablespoons of water to make a paste. Brush this over one edge of each piece of pastry, then wrap it round the fish and press to seal. The paste should stick, but if you do have trouble, secure the parcels with a little cocktail stick. Brush the parcels with olive oil.

Bake the parcels in the oven for 15 minutes until brown and crisp and serve with aïoli.

NOIX DE ST JACQUES EN CHAPELURE, AIL ET PERSIL

Scallops with Breadcrumbs, Garlic & Parsley

This is one of the simplest and most delicious ways to enjoy scallops and you don't even need a pan! Buy your scallops whole in the shells if possible and if the roes are attached and plump, you can include them in the dish. If you don't have scallop shells, heatproof dishes or ramekins will do fine.

Serves 4

8–12 SCALLOPS (DEPENDING ON SIZE), CLEANED AND TRIMMED

6 TBSP BREADCRUMBS

2 TBSP CHOPPED PARSLEY

2 GARLIC CLOVES, PEELED AND FINELY CHOPPED

2 TBSP SOFTENED BUTTER

1 LEMON, CUT INTO WEDGES

SALT AND FRESHLY GROUND BLACK PEPPER

Preheat the oven to 220°C/Fan 200°C/Gas 7 and preheat your grill.

Pat the scallops dry and arrange them on 4 shells – or use little heatproof dishes if you don't have shells.

Mix the breadcrumbs with the parsley, garlic and soft butter and season well. Divide this over the scallops.

Cook the scallops in the oven for 5 minutes, then place them under the hot grill for another 2–3 minutes to brown the breadcrumbs. Serve immediately with some lemon wedges.

BAR CUIT AUX ALGUES AVEC PURÉE DE CRESSON

Sea Bass Cooked in Seaweed with Watercress Purée

Cooking the fish with seaweed gives lovely extra flavour to this simple dish. Your fishmonger should be able to supply seaweed, or gather your own if you're at the coast. Ask your fishmonger to clean and gut the fish and trim the fins but leave the head and scales on. This adds flavour and also makes it easier to remove the skin once the fish is cooked.

Serves 2

300G SEAWEED

1 UNWAXED LEMON, SLICED

1 SEA BASS (ABOUT 800G)

1 TBSP FRESHLY GROUND BLACK PEPPER

SALT

Watercress Purée

250G WATERCRESS (TOUGH STALKS REMOVED), WASHED

30ML EXTRA VIRGIN OLIVE OIL

JUICE OF ½ LEMON

First make the watercress purée. Bring a pan of salted water to the boil, add the watercress and cook for 2 minutes. Drain, then refresh the watercress in a bowl of iced water. Drain the watercress again, then put it in a food processor or blender with the olive oil and lemon juice and blitz until smooth – you may need to add a little water. Season with a touch of salt but no pepper as watercress is naturally peppery. Set the purée aside.

Wash the seaweed, place most of it in a roasting tin and top with half the lemon slices. Season the inside of the fish with a little salt, lay it on the seaweed and lemon, then place the rest of the seaweed and lemon on top. Season with the pepper and pour in cold water to a depth of 2cm.

Tightly cover the tin with foil and place it over a high heat for 5 minutes to bring the water to the boil. Turn down the heat and leave the fish to steam gently for 20 minutes.

Remove the foil and the top layer of seaweed and carefully peel the skin off the fish. Lift the fillet off one side of the fish, then turn it over and remove the other fillet. Serve with the watercress purée and some Jersey Royal potatoes. The purée is fine cold or you can put it in a pan and gently warm it through if you prefer.

TRUITE SAUMONÉE POCHÉE

Poached Sea Trout

A farmed sea trout is best for this beautifully light fish dish, but a wild sea bass, scorpion fish or pollock can also be cooked in this way. The leftover cooking liquor makes an excellent fish stock for soups or other fish-based sauces. If you don't have a fish kettle, a deep roasting tray with a wire rack should do the trick.

Serves 6

1 SEA TROUT (ABOUT 1.75KG), CLEANED AND GUTTED

1 TBSP OLIVE OIL

1 CARROT, PEELED AND FINELY CHOPPED

1 ONION, PEELED AND FINELY CHOPPED

1 LEEK, FINELY CHOPPED

2 CELERY STICKS, FINELY CHOPPED

1 BOUQUET GARNI (SEE PAGE 8)

1 UNWAXED LEMON, THINLY SLICED

300ML DRY WHITE WINE

SALT AND FRESHLY GROUND BLACK PEPPER

Rinse the fish under cold water and pat it dry. If you're using sea bass, scale it or ask your fishmonger to do this for you.

Heat the olive oil in a frying pan. Add the vegetables and cook them until tender but don't allow them to colour.

Place the fish in a fish kettle or on a rack in a roasting tin. Season it well with salt and pepper, then add the vegetables, bouquet garni, lemon slices and wine.

Pour on enough cold water to just cover the fish. Place the pan on the hob and bring the water to a very gentle simmer, then continue to simmer for 10 minutes. Cover the kettle or roasting tin with a lid or foil, then remove it from the heat and leave the fish to rest for 10 minutes.

After 20 minutes, carefully lift the fish out of the pan. Place it on a serving dish, peel off the skin and serve it with boiled new potatoes and a light hollandaise sauce (see page 289).

SEICHE À LA SÈTOISE

Cuttlefish, Sète Style

Cuttlefish is delicious and good value for money. It's popular in France and increasingly seen in fishmongers in the UK now too. Fishmongers will usually clean the cuttlefish for you or you can do it yourself, but be prepared for a bit of mess as the ink gets everywhere! This way of cooking cuttlefish makes a great one-pot meal.

Serves 4–6

1.2KG CUTTLEFISH FLESH (CLEANED WEIGHT)

3 TBSP OLIVE OIL

2 ONIONS, PEELED AND CHOPPED

2 TBSP TOMATO PASTE

250ML DRY WHITE WINE

2 PINCHES OF SAFFRON

1 BOUQUET GARNI (MADE UP OF A BAY LEAF AND SPRIGS OF THYME, FENNEL AND PARSLEY)

6 TOMATOES, PEELED AND SEEDED

80G BLACK OLIVES, PITTED

4 TBSP AÏOLI (SEE PAGE 32)

SALT AND FRESHLY GROUND BLACK PEPPER

Cut the cuttlefish into strips of about 3 x 2cm. Warm a tablespoon of the oil in a large frying pan or sauté pan and sear the cuttlefish over a high heat to extract excess water. Drain the cuttlefish and set it aside, then discard the juices in the pan.

Heat the remaining oil in the pan and gently cook the onions until tender. Add the tomato paste and cook for 3–4 minutes, then add the wine, saffron, bouquet garni, chopped tomatoes and the olives. Simmer for another 5 minutes.

Add the cuttlefish and pour in just enough water to cover. Season well with salt and pepper. Bring to the boil, then turn the heat down to a very gentle simmer, cover the pan and cook for 60–80 minutes or until the cuttlefish is beautifully tender.

Just before serving fold in the aïoli. Serve with red Camargue rice (see page 124).

TERRINE D'OEUF NIÇOISE

Egg Terrine Niçoise

This looks spectacular but it's made with simple ingredients and, although it does take a bit of work, there's nothing difficult about it. Serve it warm from the oven or cold for a picnic or as a starter. You'll need a terrine dish or loaf tin measuring about 28 x 12cm.

Serves 6–8

4 LARGE TOMATOES, PEELED, SEEDED AND CHOPPED

1 TSP THYME LEAVES

1 SHALLOT, PEELED AND CHOPPED

2 TSP TOMATO PASTE

500G LARGE LEAF SPINACH, WASHED

1 GARLIC CLOVE, PEELED AND FINELY CHOPPED

GRATING OF NUTMEG

OLIVE OIL, FOR GREASING

12 FREE-RANGE EGGS

90ML SINGLE CREAM

75G CRUMBLY GOATS' CHEESE, GRATED

SALT AND FRESHLY GROUND BLACK PEPPER

Put the tomatoes in a pan with the thyme, shallot and tomato paste and season with salt and pepper. Cook over a medium heat for 20 minutes to get rid of the excess water, then tip everything into a bowl and set aside.

Bring a pan of salted water to the boil, add the spinach, then drain and refresh it in a bowl of iced water. Drain it again, then squeeze out as much moisture as you can. Chop the spinach, put it in a bowl and add the finely chopped garlic. Season with salt, pepper and nutmeg, then set aside.

Preheat the oven to 180°C/Fan 160°C/Gas 4 and grease the terrine dish or tin. Take the tomato mixture and beat in 4 of the eggs and 30ml of the cream, then pour the mixture into the terrine. Place the dish in a roasting tin and add just-boiled water to come halfway up the sides. Bake for 15 minutes, then remove from the oven.

Beat 4 eggs and 30ml of cream into the spinach. Carefully pour this mixture on to the tomato layer and put the terrine back in the oven for 10 minutes. Remove it from the oven.

Beat the remaining eggs with the grated cheese and the rest of the cream and pour this on top of the spinach layer. Cook for a further 20 minutes.

Leave the terrine to cool a little before serving or chill it overnight, then remove it from the dish and slice.

CHOU-FLEUR FARCI

Stuffed Cauliflower

This dish is traditionally made with cabbage but I like this cauliflower version for a welcome change. It's a real show-stopper and makes a small amount of meat go a long way.

Serves 6

1 CAULIFLOWER (ABOUT 1KG)

2 TBSP OLIVE OIL

200G BONELESS PORK SHOULDER

100G PORK FAT

1 TBSP CHOPPED PARSLEY

2 GARLIC CLOVES, PEELED AND CHOPPED

2 SLICES AIR-CURED HAM, SUCH AS BAYONNE (SEE PAGE 8)

200ML WHITE WINE

200ML CHICKEN STOCK

TOMATO COULIS (SEE PAGE 105)

SALT AND FRESHLY GROUND BLACK PEPPER

Bring a large pan of salted water to the boil and carefully add the whole cauliflower. Cook the cauliflower for 10 minutes, then drain and refresh it a bowl of iced water.

When the cauliflower is cold, drain it again really well. Remove the outer leaves, but leave the inner ones if they are nice and fresh. Using a small, sharp knife, such as a grapefruit knife, carefully cut out the central core, without breaking off any florets. Don't go too deep.

Line a bowl with a large piece of oiled foil and put the cauliflower inside, cavity-side up.

Put the pork shoulder, fat, parsley, garlic and seasoning through the finest plate of a mincer, then mix well. Preheat the oven to 220°C/Fan 200°C/Gas 7.

Fill the cavity of the cauliflower with the mince, pushing it into all the little crevices with your hands. Cover the top with the slices of ham, then fold over the foil and make sure it is really well sealed.

Place the cauliflower in a roasting tin, then add the wine and stock to the tin. Cook in the preheated oven for 30 minutes, then carefully open up the foil and continue to cook at 200°C/Fan 180°C/Gas 6, basting often, for another 45 minutes.

Gently transfer the cauliflower to a board, then whisk tomato coulis into the roasting juices. Slice the cauliflower and serve with the juices.

COURGE FARCIE CAMPAGNARDE
Stuffed Marrow with Mushrooms

Marrow can be bland but this quick and easy recipe livens it up beautifully. Serve hot with tomato coulis (see page 105) and a side salad.

Serves 4

60G DRIED CEPS

1 MARROW (500–600G)

1 TBSP OLIVE OIL

2 SHALLOTS, PEELED AND CHOPPED

2 GARLIC CLOVES, PEELED AND CHOPPED

2 TBSP BREADCRUMBS

360G MINCED PORK (OR SAUSAGEMEAT)

80G SMOKED BACON OR HAM, CHOPPED

2 TBSP CHOPPED PARSLEY

SALT AND FRESHLY GROUND BLACK PEPPER

Soak the dried mushrooms in a small bowl of warm water for about 20 minutes to reconstitute them. Drain, then chop them roughly and set aside.

Cut the marrow in half lengthways and scoop out all the seeds.

Bring a very large pan of salted water to the boil, then plunge the marrow halves into the pan and cook for 1 minute. If you don't have a pan big enough to completely submerge the marrow halves, cook them for 1 minute, then turn them and leave for another minute to blanch the other end.

Heat a tablespoon of oil in a frying pan and sweat the chopped mushrooms, shallots and garlic for 10 minutes until soft. Tip them into a bowl, season well and leave to cool slightly, then mix in the breadcrumbs, minced pork or sausagemeat, the bacon and parsley. Preheat the oven to 200°C/Fan 180°C/Gas 6.

Fill the marrow halves with the stuffing, put them in a roasting tin and bake in the oven for 35 minutes.

Heat your grill and put the marrow halves under the grill until golden on top. Slice and serve with tomato coulis (see page 105).

POULET EN GELÉE
Jellied Chicken & Bacon

This is proper French country cooking – simple ingredients but lots of flavour. Serve with a salad and grilled sourdough as a starter or with a potato salad as a summer main meal. It is vital to use stock that has lots of natural gelatine, so home-made is best (see page 284). If you don't have home-made, buy a good stock and add gelatine before using.

Serves 4

4 CHICKEN LEGS, JOINTED INTO DRUMSTICKS AND THIGHS

1 TSP CRUSHED GREEN PEPPERCORNS

2 GARLIC CLOVES, CRUSHED

1 TBSP CHOPPED PARSLEY

1 TBSP CHOPPED CHERVIL

60ML WHITE VERMOUTH

200ML DRY WHITE WINE

1.2 LITRES CHICKEN STOCK, HEATED

4 LEAVES OF GELATINE (OPTIONAL)

8 SLICES OF SMOKED STREAKY BACON

SALT

Joint the chicken legs into drumsticks and thighs or ask your butcher to do this for you.

Slash the skin of the chicken pieces several times and place them in an ovenproof dish that has a lid – I like to use an earthenware dish I can take to the table. Season the chicken with salt. Mix the peppercorns, garlic and herbs with the vermouth and wine, then pour this over the chicken and rub it in. Cover the dish and leave the chicken to marinate in the fridge for a couple of hours or overnight.

Preheat the oven to 180°C/Fan 160°C/Gas 4. Remove the chicken from the fridge and pour the hot chicken stock into the dish. Lay the slices of bacon over the chicken. If you are using bought stock, soak the leaves of gelatine for a few minutes until soft, then add them to the hot stock before using.

Cover the dish with a tight-fitting lid. You can use foil but make sure it covers the dish tightly. Put the dish in the oven and cook for 2½ hours. Remove and leave to cool, then place it in the fridge for 12 hours – the chicken will keep for 7 days.

To serve, dip the base of the dish into hot water briefly, then spoon out the chicken and jelly. The jelly should be just set.

SUPRÊMES DE VOLAILLE SAUCE BOURGUIGNONNE

Chicken Breasts with Burgundy

The chicken does have to be marinated for a couple of hours but once that's done, this is a quick dish to prepare and is ideal for a special supper.

Serves 2

500ML FULL-BODIED RED WINE (PREFERABLY BURGUNDY)

1 TBSP SUGAR

1 GARLIC CLOVE, CRUSHED

2 SKINLESS CHICKEN BREASTS, WINGLETS REMOVED

10 BUTTON ONIONS, PEELED

2 TBSP BUTTER

1 TBSP VEGETABLE OIL

10 BUTTON MUSHROOMS, WIPED

120G SMOKED BACON

300ML BROWN CHICKEN STOCK OR VEAL STOCK

SALT AND FRESHLY GROUND BLACK PEPPER

Put the red wine, sugar and garlic in a glass or ceramic bowl (the wine can react with metal) and add the chicken breasts. Cover and leave them in the fridge to marinate for 2 hours.

Put the onions in a pan of cold water and bring the water to the boil. Take the pan off the heat and drain the onions, then set them aside.

Remove the chicken and pat it dry. Pour the marinade into a pan, bring it to the boil and reduce by two-thirds.

Heat a tablespoon of the butter and the oil in a frying pan, add the chicken breasts and fry them for 15 minutes, turning them halfway through. Remove the chicken from the pan and set it aside to rest.

Add the blanched onions and the mushrooms to the frying pan and cook them for a few minutes. Drain off the excess fat, add the bacon and cook until browned. Pour the reduced marinade into the pan, add the stock and boil rapidly until the mixture is syrupy. Stir the remaining butter into the sauce.

Serve the chicken with the onion and mushroom sauce and the potato and root vegetable cake on page 199.

GÂTEAU DE LÉGUMES

Potato & Root Vegetable Cake

This is the ideal accompaniment for the chicken breasts with Burgundy (opposite), as it soaks up the lovely winey juices.

Serves 2 generously

2 FLOURY POTATOES, PEELED

1 SHALLOT, PEELED

½ CARROT, PEELED

½ PARSNIP, PEELED

1 SMALL TURNIP, PEELED

1 TBSP CHOPPED PARSLEY

2 TBSP VEGETABLE OIL

BUTTER

SALT AND FRESHLY GROUND BLACK PEPPER

Preheat the oven to 210°C/Fan 190°C/Gas 6½.

Coarsely grate all the vegetables and mix them together in a bowl. Season with salt and pepper and add the chopped parsley. Place the mixture in a clean cloth and squeeze as much water out as possible.

Heat the oil in an ovenproof 20–24cm frying pan. Tip the vegetable mixture into the pan and press it down well, then add a few knobs of butter on top. Put the pan in the oven for 15 minutes.

Remove the pan from the oven, turn the cake out on to a board and then slide it back into the pan, underside up. Put the pan back in the oven for another 10 minutes. Leave the cake to cool slightly before serving.

PINTADE AU VIEUX VINAIGRE
Guinea Fowl with Vinegar

You need good-quality vinegar for this recipe, such as a Lyonnaise or Burgundy. Guinea fowl is a favourite in France and is often served in preference to chicken for special occasions. It has a slightly stronger, gamier flavour and not as much meat on it, but it's definitely worth a try. It's a healthy meat too, as it is lean with little fat.

Serves 2 generously

2 TBSP OLIVE OIL

1 GUINEA FOWL

1 TSP TOMATO PASTE

1 CARROT, FINELY DICED

1 ONION, FINELY CHOPPED

1 CELERY STICK, FINELY DICED

4 TBSP RED WINE VINEGAR

300ML BROWN CHICKEN STOCK

1 TSP THYME LEAVES

SALT AND FRESHLY GROUND
BLACK PEPPER

Preheat the oven to 230°C/Fan 210°C/Gas 8. Rub about a tablespoon of the oil over the bird and season it well with salt and pepper.

Place the bird in a roasting tin and roast for 20 minutes, then turn the oven down to 200°C/Fan 180°C/Gas 6 and roast for a further 20 minutes. Cooking the bird at a high temperature and with little fat like this is similar to cooking on a spit and results in a crisp skin and smoky flavours.

Take the guinea fowl out of the oven, remove it from the tin and place it on a board, loosely covered with foil. Set it aside to rest for 15 minutes.

Put the roasting tin on the hob and add the remaining oil, the tomato paste and the vegetables. Cook for 2–3 minutes, then add the vinegar and stock. Boil until you have a chunky sauce, then check the seasoning and add the thyme leaves. A French bean salad (see page 66) makes a nice accompaniment.

PARMENTIER DE CONFIT DE CANARD

Duck Confit Pie

Parmentier was the man who popularised potatoes in France in the 18th century. Whenever you see his name on a dish, it will contain potatoes. This dish is a special version of cottage or shepherd's pie and very delicious. In France, you can buy confit duck legs in most butchers' shops, but if you have trouble finding them in the UK, look for vacuum-packed or canned.

Serves 4

1KG FLOURY POTATOES (KING EDWARDS OR ROOSTERS), PEELED

4 GARLIC CLOVES, LEFT WHOLE AND UNPEELED

250ML MILK

60G BUTTER

4 CONFIT DUCK LEGS

1 ONION, PEELED AND CHOPPED

2 TBSP CHOPPED PARSLEY

30G TRUFFLE, SLICED (OPTIONAL)

2 TBSP BREADCRUMBS

SALT AND FRESHLY GROUND BLACK PEPPER

Cut the potatoes into quarters. Put them in a pan of water with the garlic cloves and season with salt. Simmer until cooked, then drain, tip the potatoes and garlic back in the pan and leave them to steam and dry.

Remove the garlic, pop the skins off and put the flesh in a small pan with the milk. Simmer for 5 minutes, then blend until smooth.

Pass the potatoes through a ricer, mix in 30g of the butter and the garlicky milk, then season well. Set aside.

Preheat the oven to 200°C/Fan 180°C/Gas 6. Remove the skin and bones from the duck legs and shred the meat.

Warm a little of the fat from the confit in a frying pan and sweat the chopped onion until soft and lightly browned. Add the duck meat, parsley and the truffle, if using, and check the seasoning.

Tip the mixture into a pie dish and press it down. Spread the mashed potato on top and run a fork over it to make a pattern. Sprinkle the breadcrumbs on top and bake the pie in the oven for 20 minutes. Place the pie under a preheated grill to brown the top.

SUPRÊMES DE CANARD ET RAISINS AU GENIÈVRE

Duck Breasts with Grapes & Juniper

My version of this duck dish is rich in flavour but not in fat– there's only a small amount of cream per person. It's indulgent but not heavy. This sauce also goes well with game.

Serves 4

ABOUT 150G WHITE SEEDLESS GRAPES

4 DUCK BREASTS

2 TBSP BRANDY

120ML SWEET WINE (SUCH AS MUSCAT OR RASTEAU)

12 JUNIPER BERRIES, CRUSHED

100ML CRÈME FRAÎCHE

SALT AND FRESHLY GROUND BLACK PEPPER

Take 24 of the plumpest grapes and peel them carefully with a small sharp knife.

Blitz the remaining grapes in a food processor or a blender, then pass them through a fine sieve to get about 200ml of juice.

Score the skin of the duck breasts and place them skin-side down in a warm frying pan. Season the duck and slowly bring the heat up, then cook until the fat renders and the skin turns golden brown. Turn the breasts and cook them for a further 7–8 minutes for pink meat. Remove the duck breasts from the pan and set them aside to rest. Discard the fat.

Pour the brandy and sweet wine into the pan, bring to the boil and reduce by half. Add the grape juice and crushed juniper berries and continue to boil rapidly until again reduced by half.

Whisk in the crème fraîche, season and simmer for 2–3 minutes. Add any juices that have run from the duck and the peeled grapes to warm through.

Serve the duck breasts with the sauce and grapes and some greens, such as spinach or chard, on the side.

STEAK MINUTE

Minute Steak

A minute steak is exactly that: a steak cooked in a minute. To do this, you need a very hot pan or skillet and a thin steak at room temperature. Most cuts work, but my favourite is rib-eye, which has a nice piece of fat running through it, but flat iron and rump are also fine. Bavette or onglet is often used in France, and if you want lots of flavour and don't mind a little chewiness, is truly great.

Serves 2

2 X 120–180G STEAKS (1.5CM THICK)

2 TBSP VEGETABLE OIL

1 TBSP BUTTER

1 SHALLOT, PEELED AND FINELY CHOPPED

1 TSP CRACKED BLACK PEPPER

1 TBSP BRANDY

60ML WHITE WINE

2 TBSP CRÈME FRAÎCHE

SALT

Take the steaks out of the fridge an hour before you want to cook them to make sure they are at room temperature. Heat a heavy-based pan until it's very hot.

Brush the steaks with oil on both sides and season them with a little salt. Place them in the pan and let them sear for 20 seconds – don't shake the pan or prod the meat. Turn the steaks and continue to cook for 30 or so seconds, then add the butter and baste. The steaks should be nicely seared and even a little charred.

Take the steaks out of the pan and leave them on a plate to rest.

Add the shallot to the pan, followed by the pepper, then stir and cook for 15 seconds. Pour in the brandy and wine, which should boil immediately. Add the crème fraîche and take the pan off the heat. Pour any juices from the resting steak into the sauce. Serve the steaks with the sauce and a salad.

JARRET DE BOEUF EN COCOTTE
Pot-Roast Beef Shin

Slow cooking turns this cheap cut of beef into a feast – soft, tender and full of flavour. It's a great alternative to roast beef and it's cooked in one pot so very easy to prepare. Ask your butcher to bone and tie the meat for you.

Serves 8

1 BEEF SHIN (ABOUT 2.8KG), BONE IN, TRIMMED AND TIED

10 GARLIC CLOVES, PEELED

3 ONIONS, PEELED AND SLICED

1 ROSEMARY SPRIG

2 BAY LEAVES

50ML BRANDY

500ML RED WINE

4 TBSP OLIVE OIL

2 LITRES VEAL OR BEEF STOCK

SALT AND FRESHLY GROUND BLACK PEPPER

Put the beef in a large, deep bowl and add the garlic, onions, herbs, brandy and wine. Roll the beef in this marinade, then cover the bowl and leave it in the fridge for 8–12 hours. Turn the meat at least once to ensure the marinade gets to all parts.

Drain the shin and the vegetables and herbs, and reserve the liquid. Pat the meat dry. Heat the oil in a large flameproof casserole dish and sear the beef on all sides – it's very important to get it well caramelised.

Set the beef aside, then put the vegetables and herbs from the marinade in the dish and cook until they're well caramelised. This will take about 20 minutes – keep scraping the bottom of the pan to lift off all the sugars. Preheat the oven to 190°C/Fan 170°C/Gas 5.

Pour the reserved marinade liquid into the dish, bring to the boil and reduce by half. Add the stock and the beef, season with salt and pepper, then bring to a simmer. Place a lid on the dish, put it in the oven and cook for 3 hours, turning the meat after 1½ hours. Leave to cool a little before serving with mashed potatoes.

If you want a slightly more elegant sauce, remove the meat from the casserole dish once it is cooked and set it aside. Pass the cooking liquid and vegetables through a sieve back into the dish, pressing well to mash the vegetables and thicken the sauce. Bring the liquid back to the boil and serve with the meat.

CARRÉ D'AGNEAU EN CROÛTE D'OLIVE

Rack of Lamb with an Olive Crust

Straight out of Provence, this rack of lamb dish is good served with braised fennel and some roasted new potatoes. Rack is a prime cut – pricey but ideal for a special treat.

Serves 4-6

60G PITTED GREEN OLIVES

40G GROUND ALMONDS

30G BREADCRUMBS

ZEST AND JUICE OF 1 LEMON

2 TBSP OLIVE OIL

1 GARLIC CLOVE, PEELED AND CHOPPED

1 TBSP CHOPPED PARSLEY

2 RACKS OF LAMB (FRENCH TRIMMED)

SALT AND FRESHLY GROUND BLACK PEPPER

Braised Fennel

2 FENNEL BULBS

2 TBSP OLIVE OIL

2 TBSP PASTIS

1 TSP FENNEL SEEDS

JUICE OF 1 LEMON

200ML VEGETABLE OR CHICKEN STOCK

SALT AND FRESHLY GROUND BLACK PEPPER

Place all the ingredients for the lamb, except for the meat, in a food processor and blend until smooth. The mixture should come together as a paste. Preheat the oven to 220°C/Fan 200°C/Gas 7.

Season the racks, then place them fat-side down in a pan over a medium heat to render the fat and brown the skin. When the racks are nicely brown, take the pan off the heat. Turn the racks over and spread the olive paste all over the browned meat and skin, then transfer them to a roasting tin.

Roast the lamb racks for 12 minutes for pink meat. Take them out and leave them to rest for 7–8 minutes before carving.

Meanwhile, trim the fennel bulbs and cut them into quarters. Heat the oil in a pan and carefully fry the fennel on all sides until lightly coloured. Add the pastis, followed by the fennel seeds, lemon juice and stock.

Season and simmer until the fennel is tender and the liquid has almost completely evaporated, then serve with the lamb.

HARICOT DE MOUTON
Lamb with Haricot Beans

This was traditionally made with mutton and it's just as good with hogget or lamb – but not spring lamb. It's really a French version of Lancashire hotpot and a good hearty, healthy meal, all in one pot.

Serves 6

500G DRIED HARICOT BEANS

2 ONIONS, PEELED AND DICED

1 BAY LEAF

4 GARLIC CLOVES, PEELED AND CRUSHED

2 BOUQUETS GARNIS

4 TBSP VEGETABLE OIL

1.2KG BONED LAMB NECK OR SHOULDER, CUT INTO 4CM PIECES

2 CARROTS, PEELED AND DICED

2 TBSP TOMATO PASTE

SALT AND FRESHLY GROUND BLACK PEPPER

Soak the beans in cold water overnight. Drain them, put them in a pan with half the diced onions and the bay leaf, then cover generously with cold water. Add 2 of the garlic cloves and a bouquet garni and bring to the boil. Simmer for 45 minutes or until almost tender – the beans will be cooked again later. Drain the beans and set them and the cooking liquid aside.

Heat 2 tablespoons of the oil in a large flameproof casserole dish and sear the meat until golden. It's best to do this in batches so as not to overcrowd the pan. Remove each batch as it is browned.

Discard any fat in the pan. Add the rest of the oil and cook the remaining onion and garlic with the carrots over a medium heat until lightly coloured.

Add the tomato paste and the remaining bouquet garni and stir, scraping the bottom of the pan well. Put the meat back in the pan with enough of the bean cooking liquid to cover. Season, cover the pan and simmer gently for 45 minutes. Add the beans with more water if needed and simmer for a further 30 minutes. Serve in wide bowls.

DESSERTS

Puddings

I have to admit I have a sweet tooth and I do like to finish a meal with a little something, even it is only a delicious biscuit with my coffee. French desserts can be complex and calorific but most of the recipes in this chapter are simple to make and not heavy. They range from easy compotes to dainty fruit tarts – something for every occasion.

TARTE TATIN AUX FIGUES
Fig Tarte Tatin

The classic recipe is with apple, but tarte tatin can be made with all sorts of fruits and I think this fig version is particularly good.

Serves 4

35G BUTTER

70G GOLDEN CASTER SUGAR

PINCH OF SEA SALT

12 FRESH FIGS, CUT IN HALF

250G PUFF PASTRY

Melt the butter, sugar and salt in a frying pan. When the mixture is bubbling, add the figs and cook them for 5 minutes over a high heat, turning them over after 2½ minutes.

Transfer the figs and juices to a tarte tatin pan or an ovenproof dish that's about 20cm wide. Leave to cool. Preheat the oven to 210°C/190°C/Gas 6½.

Roll out the pastry to a circle about 3cm wider than the pan. Place this on top of the figs, tucking in the excess pastry around them.

Cut 8 little holes in the pastry with the point of a knife. Bake the tart in the oven for 35 minutes, then remove it and leave it to cool slightly.

To turn the tart out, take a plate of about the same size as the pan and place it over the pan. Quickly turn the pan over to transfer the tart to the plate.

PAIN PERDU À LA NORMANDE
French Toast, Normandy Style

Sometimes you need a pudding that is unashamedly luxurious and this is it. However, it does use up stale bread and it's quick to make for a once-in-a-while treat.

Serves 2

1 FREE-RANGE EGG

125ML MILK

1 TSP GROUND CINNAMON

4 TBSP SUGAR

2 THICK SLICES OF STALE BREAD OR BRIOCHE

3 TBSP BUTTER

2 EATING APPLES

CALVADOS

150ML WHIPPING CREAM

1 TBSP ICING SUGAR

Mix the egg, milk and cinnamon with a tablespoon of the sugar in a bowl. Dunk the slices of bread into this mixture to moisten them.

Heat a tablespoon of the butter in a pan. Take the slices of bread out of the milk mixture and place them in the hot pan with the butter. Brown the bread on both sides, then add a tablespoon of sugar to the pan and another tablespoon of butter to caramelise. Take the slices of bread out and set them aside.

Cut one and a half of the apples into wedges – no need to peel them. Heat the rest of the butter and sugar in the pan and fry the apples until they are just cooked and browned. Add a good splash of Calvados and then set the pan aside.

Whisk the cream with the icing sugar. Cut the remaining apple half into thin matchsticks.

Divide the warm apples between the slices of bread, spoon on some cream and sprinkle a few strips of raw apple on top. Serve at once!

CLAFOUTIS AUX PRUNEAUX
Prune Clafoutis

You can make this great French classic with a host of different fruit, but I like to cook this version with prunes in winter, when there is less fresh fruit about. I always keep an airtight container full of prunes plumped up with brandy and they are what I use here. The ground almonds aren't traditional but I find they add good flavour and texture. You can vary the spices – cinnamon is good but vanilla seeds or star anise are other options.

Serves 8

200ML MILK

60ML DOUBLE CREAM

2 CINNAMON STICKS

24 PITTED PRUNES, MARINATED IN BRANDY

4 FREE-RANGE EGGS

30G PLAIN FLOUR

30G GROUND ALMONDS

160G CASTER SUGAR

1 TBSP BUTTER

Preheat the oven to 200°C/Fan 180°C/Gas 6. Bring the milk and cream to the boil with the cinnamon sticks, then take the pan off the heat and set it aside.

Cut the prunes in half and add a couple of spoonfuls of the brandy to the milk mixture.

Whisk the eggs in a bowl with the flour, ground almonds and 130g of the sugar, then stir in the milk and cream to make a batter and set aside.

Grease a ceramic flan dish with the butter and sprinkle over the remaining sugar. Arrange the prunes in the dish, then pour in the batter.

Cook in the preheated oven for 10 minutes, then turn the heat down to 180°C/Fan 160°C/Gas 4 and cook for a further 20 minutes. Serve warm.

SOUPE DE FRUITS ROUGES
À LA VERVEINE
Fruit Soup with Verbena

This beautiful, verbena-flavoured dessert is summer in a bowl. And it is even better with a few little madeleines (see page 254) on the side.

Serves 4

75G CASTER SUGAR

2 TBSP BLOSSOM HONEY

2 FRESH VERBENA SPRIGS
(OR A HANDFUL OF DRIED)

500G MIXED BERRIES (STRAWBERRIES, RASPBERRIES, BLACKBERRIES, REDCURRANTS, BLACKCURRANTS)

FRESHLY GROUND BLACK PEPPER
(OPTIONAL)

Pour 500ml of water into a pan, add the sugar and honey and bring to the boil.

Add the verbena and simmer for 2 minutes. Take the pan off the heat, cover and leave to infuse for about 10 minutes. Remove the verbena.

Pour the liquid into a bowl, add the fruit, then leave to cool. Chill the soup in the fridge until it is very cold.

Just before serving I like to add a little freshly ground black pepper.

COMPOTE DES FRUITS
Fruit Compotes

I was brought up on these. All through the year there is fruit that can be cooked and mashed up into a delicious sweet compote. The amount of sugar added really depends on the fruit and its natural sugar level – and your own taste – so adapt as you wish. These compotes can be kept in the fridge for a week to ten days and are lovely served with yoghurt or cream.

Serves 6

Apple Compote

3 SHARP COOKING APPLES

6 EATING APPLES

80G CASTER SUGAR

JUICE OF 1 LEMON

1 CINNAMON STICK

Apricot Compote

30 APRICOTS

180G CASTER SUGAR

2 VANILLA PODS

1 TSP ALMOND EXTRACT (OPTIONAL)

For the apple compote, I like to peel the apples but some people, like my wife, prefer not to! Up to you.

Core and cut the apples into small pieces, put them in a pan and add the sugar, lemon juice and cinnamon stick. Cover and bring to a gentle simmer for 20 minutes. Remove the cinnamon to serve. Nice drizzled with a little honey if you like.

For the apricot compote, cut the apricots in half and discard the stones. Place the apricots in a pan with the sugar. Scrape the seeds from the halved vanilla pods into the pan and add a couple of tablespoons of water. Cover and bring to a gentle simmer for 20 minutes, then add the almond extract, if using.

I like this compote smooth so I blitz it in a food processor before serving, but you can leave it chunky if you prefer.

SALADE DE FRUITS

Fruit Salad

Fruit salad is such a wonderful way to end a meal but deserves to be carefully made. There should be a balance of sweetness, acidity and, of course, textures, and I like to add a little kick in the form of some eau de vie or kirsch. Serving fruit salad in a hollowed-out watermelon is a bit of theatre to try when you want to make something a bit more special. Nice served with some palmiers (see page 252) or speculoos biscuits (see page 251).

Serves 6–8

1 SMALL WATERMELON

2 TBSP CASTER SUGAR

200G STRAWBERRIES, HULLED

100G BLACKBERRIES

100G BLACKCURRANTS

6 APRICOTS, STONED AND QUARTERED

6 PLUMS, STONED AND QUARTERED

4 TBSP EAU DE VIE (OPTIONAL)

Dice the watermelon flesh and put it in a bowl with the rest of the fruit. Sprinkle on the sugar and add the alcohol, if using, then cover the bowl and put it in the fridge. After 30 minutes, carefully toss the fruit to mix it with the sugar, then serve.

If you want to serve the salad in the melon, slice the top off the melon and hollow it out, removing any seeds. Dice the flesh and proceed as above. Fill the melon with the fruit and take it to the table.

MOUSSE AU CHOCOLAT
Chocolate Mousse

Simple and quick to make, this is a true French staple with only 3 ingredients. There's no cream, no butter, a small amount of sugar – but lots of chocolate! This recipe does contain raw eggs.

Serves 6–8

220G DARK CHOCOLATE (70% COCOA SOLIDS), BROKEN INTO PIECES

8 FREE-RANGE EGGS

2 TBSP CASTER SUGAR

COARSE SEA SALT (OPTIONAL)

Set a heatproof bowl over a saucepan of simmering water, making sure the bottom of the bowl doesn't touch the water.

Add the chocolate to the bowl with 2 tablespoons of water, and allow it to melt slowly, making sure it doesn't overheat. Once melted, set the bowl of chocolate aside to cool slightly.

Separate the eggs, making sure the whites go in a scrupulously clean bowl with no trace of fat or they won't whisk properly. Whisk the egg yolks into the cooled chocolate.

Add the sugar to the egg whites and beat them with an electric hand beater until stiff. Fold them into the chocolate a little at a time. I like to add just a pinch of coarse sea salt to bring out the flavour of the chocolate.

Spoon the mixture into little cups or glass bowls and refrigerate for a couple of hours before serving.

GLACE AU CHOCOLAT
Chocolate Ice Cream

Chocolate ice cream is my very favourite and this is an easy one to make. There is quite a bit of whisking to do but you don't need an ice-cream maker and there's no need to keep taking the mixture out of the freezer to stir. Just freeze it and enjoy.

Serves 6-8

50G MILK CHOCOLATE

250ML DOUBLE CREAM

160G DARK CHOCOLATE (70% COCOA SOLIDS), BROKEN INTO PIECES

2 FREE-RANGE EGGS, PLUS 1 YOLK

90G CASTER SUGAR

1 TSP VANILLA EXTRACT

Chop or coarsely grate the milk chocolate and put it in the fridge to keep cold. Whisk the cream in a bowl until it holds firm peaks.

Put the dark chocolate in a bowl over a pan of simmering water, making sure the bottom of the bowl doesn't touch the water. Allow the chocolate to melt — don't let it overheat — then carefully remove the bowl from the pan and set it aside.

Place the eggs, egg yolk, sugar and vanilla in another bowl and set it over the pan of simmering water. Whisk the mixture with a balloon whisk for 10 minutes until it is pale and frothy. Be sure to keep the temperature low or the eggs will scramble. This process partially cooks the eggs and sets the mixture, giving a lovely creamy texture to the ice cream.

Take the pan off the heat and carefully remove the bowl, then mix in the melted dark chocolate. Leave the mixture to cool a little, then fold in the whipped cream and grated milk chocolate.

Tip the mixture into a airtight freezer-proof container and freeze for about 8 hours before serving.

GLACE AU YAOURT ET FRAISE
Yoghurt & Strawberry Ice Cream

This is such a simple ice cream – again, no machine needed. I like strawberry jam in this, but you can use another kind if you prefer. I also like to garnish the ice cream with some toasted nuts, such as pistachios and sliced almonds.

Serves 4

500G PLAIN YOGHURT

100G STRAWBERRY JAM

100ML DOUBLE CREAM

JUICE AND ZEST OF 1 LEMON

PISTACHIOS AND SLICED ALMONDS
(OPTIONAL)

Blitz all the ingredients, except the nuts, in a food processor until smooth. Scoop the mixture into an airtight freezer-proof container. Place it in the freezer and leave for 6–8 hours.

Toast the nuts, if using, in a dry pan until golden, then set them aside. Serve the ice cream topped with the toasted nuts.

PÊCHES POCHÉES AU ROMARIN

Poached Peaches with Rosemary

Rosemary and peaches go so well together and this is great with all varieties of peach – white, yellow, red or nectarines. Any leftover poaching syrup makes great champagne cocktails or you can mix it with some tea to make the most delicious iced tea.

Serves 6

6 PEACHES

1KG CASTER SUGAR

2 ROSEMARY SPRIGS

If, like me, you are not a fan of peach skin, blanch the peaches first and peel off the skin. Cut a small cross in the base of each peach. Bring a pan of water to the boil, add the peaches and leave them for 30 seconds, then remove and put them in a bowl of cold water. Peel off the skins.

Fill a large pan with 2 litres of water and add the sugar and rosemary. Bring to the boil, add the peaches and simmer them for 20 minutes – put a piece of baking paper over them to keep them down in the water. Remove the pan from the heat and leave to cool.

Serve the peaches with a little of the poaching syrup.

POIRES RÔTIS AUX NOUGAT ET SAUCE CHOCOLAT

Roast Pears with Nougat & Dark Chocolate Sauce

This is such a good dessert and is simple to make – you can use shop-bought nougat which, when cooked, has the same texture as toasted marshmallows. Any type of pear is fine, as long as they are ripe. The chocolate sauce is made without dairy fats and only sweetened with maple syrup – it's great with ice cream too.

Serves 4

2 RIPE PEARS, PEELED AND CORED

1 TBSP BUTTER, MELTED

200G NOUGAT

Chocolate Sauce

2 TBSP MAPLE SYRUP

2 TBSP COCOA POWDER

100G DARK CHOCOLATE (70% COCOA SOLIDS), BROKEN INTO PIECES

Preheat the oven to 200°C/Fan 180°C/Gas 6. Cut the pears in half, put them in a baking dish and brush them with a little melted butter. Cut the nougat into chunks and scatter them over the pears. Roast the pears in the oven for about 12 minutes or until golden and tender.

For the sauce, put the syrup and cocoa powder in a pan and add 100ml of water. Bring to the boil, while whisking. Add the chocolate and stir until it melts.

Serve the sauce with the pears.

TARTLELETTES AUX FRUITS ROUGES
Fruit Tarts

Vary the fruit for these little tarts as you like, but always make sure it is ripe and seasonal. I enjoy arranging the fruit prettily or you can just pile it on if you prefer. I usually make round tarts, but you can also make boat-shaped ones in special barquette moulds.

Serves 8

250G SWEET PASTRY (SEE PAGE 295)

500G FRUIT, SUCH AS STRAWBERRIES, RASPBERRIES, BLACKBERRIES, REDCURRANTS

Sweet Almond Paste

80G BUTTER, SOFTENED

80G CASTER SUGAR

100G GROUND ALMONDS

1 PINCH OF SALT

2 FREE-RANGE EGGS

1 TBSP DARK RUM

To Glaze (optional)

MELTED APRICOT JAM

ICING SUGAR

Preheat the oven to 200°C/Fan 180°C/Gas 6. Roll out the pastry to a thickness of 5mm and cut out shapes to line your tart moulds.

To make the almond paste, place the butter, sugar, ground almonds and salt in a food processor and blitz until the mixture is pale and well combined. Add the eggs, one at a time, then add the rum, and blitz again.

Spoon the almond paste into the tarts to fill them three-quarters full. Cook the tarts for 20 minutes until golden brown and fully cooked. Remove them from the oven and leave them to cool.

Arrange the fruit on top. Do this just before serving, otherwise the fruit may soften the pastry. If desired, glaze the tarts with melted apricot jam or sprinkle with icing sugar.

TOURMENT D'AMOUR

Guadeloupe Pastries

These are delicate sweet pastries, originally from Les Saintes archipelago, Guadeloupe, but now found all over the French West Indies. Traditionally, they were made by fishermen's wives as a treat for their husbands on their safe return. You'll need eight tartlet moulds, about 9 x 5cm.

Serves 8

300G SWEET PASTRY (SEE PAGE 295)

Coconut Jam

80G DESICCATED COCONUT

JUICE AND ZEST OF 2 LIMES

1 TSP GROUND CINNAMON

30G BROWN SUGAR

1 RIPE BANANA, MASHED

Crème Pâtissière

2 FREE-RANGE EGG YOLKS

50G CASTER SUGAR

30G CORNFLOUR

1 TSP VANILLA EXTRACT

1 TBSP DARK RUM

250ML MILK

Genoise Sponge

3 FREE-RANGE EGGS

90G CASTER SUGAR

90G PLAIN FLOUR, SIFTED

Put the coconut in a pan and add lukewarm water to come level. Leave it to soak for an hour.

Add the other ingredients for the coconut jam, including the mashed banana, and simmer gently for 30 minutes. Stir regularly so the mixture doesn't catch on the base of the pan. The coconut jam should be thick, sticky and light golden in colour. Leave it to cool.

For the crème pâtissière, whisk the yolks, sugar, cornflour, vanilla extract and rum together in a bowl until pale. Bring the milk to the boil in a pan, then pour the boiling milk into the egg mixture. Mix well, then tip it all back into the pan. Bring to the boil, then take the pan off the heat and set aside to cool.

Preheat the oven to 200°C/Fan 180°C/Gas 6. Roll out the sweet pastry and cut out circles to fit your moulds. Line the moulds with sweet pastry. Add a good tablespoon of coconut jam, followed by 2 generous spoonfuls of crème pâtissière to each pastry case.

For the sponge, whisk the eggs and sugar in a bowl until pale and firm (this will take about 10 minutes), then fold in the sifted flour. Divide the sponge mixture between the moulds.

Bake the pastries in the oven for 35–40 minutes. Leave them to cool a little before serving – if you can!

BOULANGERIE

Cakes, Biscuits & Bread

Baguettes aren't the only type of bread we eat in France and in this chapter I've included some easy but tasty breads, using ingredients such as chestnut flour. You'll also find some cakes and biscuits — not the exquisite creations you see in the windows of patisseries in France but light and simple recipes that can be served as a snack or dessert.

CAKE AU CITRON

Lemon Cake

This simple cake is as popular in France as it is in England, but we serve it plain, without sweet lemon icing. Candied lemon peel can be bought in most good supermarkets or delis, but the recipe works fine without it if you can't find any.

Makes 10 slices

75G BUTTER, SOFTENED,
PLUS EXTRA FOR GREASING

200ML CRÈME FRAÎCHE

150G CASTER SUGAR

3 LARGE FREE-RANGE EGGS

220G PLAIN FLOUR

2 TSP BAKING POWDER

20G CANDIED LEMON PEEL (OPTIONAL)

ZEST AND JUICE OF 1 UNWAXED LEMON

Preheat the oven to 200°C/Fan 180°C/Gas 6. Grease a 450g loaf tin and line it with baking paper.

Using an electric hand whisk, beat the softened butter, crème fraîche and sugar in a bowl until creamy. Add the eggs one at a time, whisking well.

Mix the flour, baking powder, lemon juice and zest and the chopped peel, if using, in a bowl, then fold this into the wet ingredients. Pour the mixture into the prepared loaf tin and bake for 40 minutes.

Remove the cake from the oven and leave it to cool in the tin for 5 minutes. Turn it out on to a wire rack to finish cooling.

CAKE AUX FRUITS

Fruit Cake

French fruit cake is much lighter than its British counterpart, but it doesn't last as long and goes stale after about a week. Enjoy it while it's fresh and delicious! You may be surprised at the initial high oven temperature, but starting the baking like this helps to set the fruit nicely so it doesn't all sink to the bottom.

Makes 1 x 28cm cake

250G MIXED DRIED FRUIT (SULTANAS, CURRANTS, RAISINS, PEEL)

100ML RUM OR KIRSCH

500G SOFTENED BUTTER, PLUS EXTRA FOR GREASING

300G CASTER SUGAR

2 FREE-RANGE EGGS

4 FREE-RANGE EGGS, SEPARATED

2 TSP BAKING POWDER

500G PLAIN FLOUR

½ TSP SALT

To decorate (optional)

APRICOT JAM, WARMED

GLACÉ FRUIT

The night before you want to make the cake, put the dried fruit in a bowl with the rum or Kirsch and leave it to macerate.

Grease a 28cm cake tin and line it with baking paper. Preheat the oven to 240°C/Fan 220°C/Gas 9.

Using an electric whisk, beat the butter and sugar in a bowl until light and fluffy, then gradually add 2 whole eggs and 4 additional egg yolks. Keep whisking for about 6 minutes, until the mixture is pale.

Mix the baking powder with the flour and fold this into the butter, sugar and egg mixture. Fold in the soaked fruit and liquor.

Whisk the 4 egg whites with the salt in a clean bowl until they form stiff peaks, then fold them into the mixture. Pour the mixture into the prepared tin and place it in the hot oven for 5 minutes. Then turn the oven down to 200°C/Fan 180°C/Gas 6 and bake the cake for a further 45 minutes – cover the cake with some foil after about 10 minutes so the top doesn't get too dark.

At the end of the cooking time, insert a skewer into the cake – if it comes out clean the cake is ready. If not, bake for another 5 minutes. Leave the cake to cool in the tin, then turn it out on to a wire rack. If you like, you can brush the cake with some warmed apricot jam and then decorate it with some glacé fruit.

SABLÉ BRETON
Brittany Shortbread

This delicate shortbread is very buttery and delicious. It's a speciality of Brittany, perfect with a coffee or with a dessert such as a fruit compote or frozen yoghurt.

Makes 35 biscuits

200G BUTTER

120G CASTER SUGAR AND 1 TBSP
GRANULATED SUGAR

3 FREE-RANGE EGG YOLKS

1 TSP VANILLA EXTRACT

PINCH OF SEA SALT

280G PLAIN FLOUR, PLUS EXTRA
FOR DUSTING

Using an electric whisk, beat the butter and caster sugar together in a bowl for 2–3 minutes until light and fluffy. Add 2 of the egg yolks, the vanilla and salt, then fold in the flour. Do not overwork the mixture. Wrap it in cling film and chill it in the fridge for half an hour to firm up.

Preheat the oven to 210°C/Fan 190°C/Gas 6½. Roll out the dough on a lightly floured work surface to about to 1cm thick, then cut into small rounds about 4cm in diameter. Place them on a baking tray. Beat the remaining egg yolk with a little water, then brush the biscuits with this mixture. Make little indentations in the top of each one with the back of a fork and sprinkle them with the granulated sugar.

Bake the biscuits for 12–15 minutes until golden. Transfer them to a wire rack to cool, then store in an airtight tin.

GÂTEAU AU YAOURT
Yoghurt Cake

This simple cake is child's play – in fact it's often one of the first recipes that a French child cooks at home with the family. There's no need to weigh anything, as you just use the yoghurt pot to measure the rest of the ingredients.

Makes 10 slices

1 X 125G POT OF PLAIN YOGHURT

1 POT OF VEGETABLE OIL, PLUS EXTRA FOR GREASING

1 POT OF FREE-RANGE EGGS (USUALLY 2 LARGE EGGS)

2 POTS OF CASTER SUGAR

3 POTS OF PLAIN FLOUR

1 TSP BAKING POWDER

1 TSP VANILLA ESSENCE OR GRATED LEMON ZEST

Lightly grease a silicone mould or a loaf tin. Preheat the oven to 200°C/Fan 180°C/Gas 6.

Whisk the yoghurt, oil and eggs together in a bowl, then stir in the remaining ingredients. Don't overwork the mixture. Pour the mixture into the prepared tin and bake for 35–40 minutes.

Remove the cake from the oven and leave it to cool in the tin for 5 minutes. Transfer it to a wire rack to finish cooling.

You can also make small cakes in muffin tins. Bake these for about 20 minutes.

SPECULOOS

Spicy Biscuits

These delicious spice-laden biscuits are made all over Flanders, Holland and Germany and are also popular in France. They keep for ages in an airtight tin and are a perfect accompaniment to light fruit desserts. You can vary the spices, but I find that including some ground ginger gives a really lovely warm kick of flavour.

Makes about 30

150G BUTTER, SOFTENED

200G SOFT BROWN SUGAR (PREFERABLY MUSCOVADO)

1 TBSP GROUND CINNAMON

2 TSP GROUND GINGER

1 TSP GROUND NUTMEG

½ TSP GROUND CLOVES

½ TSP SALT

3 FREE-RANGE EGGS

500G PLAIN FLOUR

1 TSP BAKING POWDER

Whisk the butter with the sugar, spices and salt in a bowl until pale and creamy. Add the eggs one at a time, whisking in between each one.

Mix the flour and baking powder in a bowl, then gradually fold them into the egg mixture to make a smooth dough. Wrap the dough in cling film and leave it to rest in the fridge for 2 hours.

Preheat the oven to 180°C/Fan 160°C/Gas 4. Roll the dough out to 5mm thick and cut it into rectangles or whatever shape you prefer. If you like, score a pattern on the biscuits with the tip of a sharp knife.

Place the biscuits on a baking tray and bake for 20–25 minutes. Remove them from the oven and leave them to cool on the baking tray for 10 minutes. Transfer them to a wire rack to cool completely. Store the biscuits in an airtight jar or tin.

PALMIERS ET SACRISTAINS
Sweet Pastries

These are for lovers of puff pastry. They're a perfect accompaniment to most desserts or delicious just on their own.

Makes about 20

60G CASTER SUGAR

200G QUICK PUFF PASTRY (SEE PAGE 296)

PALMIERS

Sprinkle a little sugar on your work surface and over the pastry. Roll the pastry out into a neat rectangle measuring about 36 × 20cm.

Fold the 2 shorter edges in to join in the middle. Sprinkle the pastry with more sugar and fold the 2 short edges in again. Pressing down slightly with the rolling pin, repeat the fold. Press with the rolling pin again, then fold the pastry in half. Wrap the pastry in cling film and leave it in the fridge for a couple of hours.

When you're nearly ready to bake the palmiers, preheat the oven to 230°C/Fan 210°C/Gas 8. Cut the pastry into slices 1cm thick and place them on a baking sheet, cut-side down. Bake the pastries for 10 minutes, then flip them over and bake for another 10 minutes. Place them on a wire rack to cool.

Makes 10–12

200G QUICK PUFF PASTRY (SEE PAGE 296)

20G CASTER SUGAR

1 FREE-RANGE EGG YOLK

40G NIBBED ALMONDS

SACRISTAINS

Preheat the oven to 220°C/Fan 200°C/Gas 7. Dust the pastry with caster sugar on both sides, then roll it out to about 5mm thick. Mix the egg yolk with 2 tablespoons of water and brush this all over the pastry. Sprinkle the almonds over the pastry and gently press them down.

Cut the pastry into strips 2cm wide and at least 12cm long. Twist each one 3 times to make a spiral and place them on a baking sheet, pressing them down lightly at each end. Bake for 20 minutes, then cool on a wire rack.

MADELEINES

Buttery French Cakes

These dainty little cakes are gorgeous just out of the oven but you can make them in advance. They also freeze very well once cooked – just put them in a warm oven to heat through. Ideally, bake your madeleines in the traditional scallop-shaped moulds but you could also use fairy cake tins.

Makes 12–16

100G BUTTER, MELTED AND COOLED, PLUS EXTRA FOR GREASING

100G PLAIN FLOUR, PLUS EXTRA FOR DUSTING

2 FREE-RANGE EGGS

100G CASTER SUGAR

¾ TBSP BAKING POWDER

ZEST OF 1 UNWAXED LEMON

Brush the madeleine trays with a little melted butter. Shake in a little flour to coat, tapping out the excess.

Whisk the eggs and sugar in a bowl until the mixture is really light and frothy. Gently whisk in the flour and baking powder, followed by the lemon zest and butter. Leave the mixture to rest for 20 minutes. Preheat the oven to 220°C/Fan 200°C/Gas 7.

Carefully spoon the mixture into the prepared moulds. Bake the cakes for 8–10 minutes until they have risen nicely and are firm to the touch. Tap them out of the tray on to a wire rack to cool briefly before devouring!

GALETTES DE SARRASIN

Buckwheat Pancakes

Popular in Brittany, galettes can be sweet or savoury but they are always a treat. You can fill them with anything you like to make a quick snack or a meal. Here are a couple of ideas.

Serves 2

Pancakes

100G BUCKWHEAT FLOUR

1 PINCH OF SALT

1 TBSP BUTTER, MELTED

1 FREE-RANGE EGG

300ML MILK

1 TBSP VEGETABLE OIL

Savoury Galette

1 TSP WHOLEGRAIN MUSTARD

2 TBSP VEGETABLE OIL

2 TSP RED WINE VINEGAR

HANDFUL OF MIXED BABY LEAF SALAD

4 SLICES OF HAM

10 WALNUT KERNELS

SALT AND FRESHLY GROUND
BLACK PEPPER

Sweet Galette

1 TBSP STRAWBERRY JAM

100G PLAIN YOGHURT

125G STRAWBERRIES, BLUEBERRIES
OR RASPBERRIES

Whisk the flour, salt, melted butter, egg and half the milk in a bowl to make a smooth paste, then mix in the remaining milk.

Heat a pan with a smear of oil. Spoon in just enough batter to cover the base of the pan and cook until the underside is golden. Flip it over to cook the other side, then remove the pancake and keep it warm. Continue until you have used all the batter.

SAVOURY GALETTE

Mix the mustard, oil and vinegar to make a dressing, season with salt and pepper, then dress the salad leaves. Fill the pancakes with the ham and salad and sprinkle with the walnuts, then roll them up and serve.

SWEET GALETTE

Stir the jam through the yoghurt so you get a ripple effect, then drizzle the mixture over the pancakes. Add the berries, roll the pancakes up and serve.

PAIN AU FROMAGE DE CHÈVRE

Goats' Cheese Bread

This herby cheese bread is a great way of using up odds and ends of goats' cheese – the drier the better. Lovely served with a bowl of soup for lunch.

Makes 1 loaf

15G FRESH YEAST OR 7G DRIED

250ML LUKEWARM WATER

80G COOKED MASHED POTATO

2½ TSP SALT

600G SPELT FLOUR

75G DRY GOATS' CHEESE, COARSELY GRATED

1 TBSP THYME AND ROSEMARY LEAVES

2 TBSP OLIVE OIL

Dissolve the yeast in the water, then add the mashed potato, salt and flour. Knead for 10 minutes until you have a smooth, elastic dough. Put the dough in a bowl, cover and leave it to rise in a warm place until doubled in volume.

Once the dough has doubled in size, knock it back and knead in the grated cheese and the herbs. Shape the dough into a freeform loaf – a focaccia shape works well – and brush it with olive oil. Cover and leave to rise again until doubled in size.

Preheat the oven to 240°C/Fan 220°C/Gas 9. Put the loaf on a baking sheet and bake for 30–35 minutes.

GOUGÈRES

Choux Cheese Pastries

Choux pastry is a cornerstone of French patisserie and it's wonderful as a savoury or sweet dish. This classic savoury version hails from Burgundy. I like to use Comté cheese but any good tangy hard cheese will work. When freshly baked, the gougères are good just as they are. But if you wish to be more indulgent, fill them with the fromage blanc or with mornay sauce (see page 290).

Makes 25–35

Choux Pastry

120ML WHOLE MILK

1 TSP SALT

1 TSP SUGAR

110G BUTTER

140G PLAIN FLOUR

5 FREE-RANGE EGGS

80G HARD CHEESE, GRATED

Fromage Blanc Filling

200G FROMAGE BLANC (LIGHT CREAM CHEESE)

1 TBSP CHOPPED CHIVES

1 TBSP CHOPPED TARRAGON

40G SMOKED HAM, CHOPPED

SALT AND FRESHLY GROUND BLACK PEPPER

Preheat the oven to 240°C/Fan 220°C/Gas 9. Pour the milk into a saucepan and add the salt, sugar, butter and 120ml of water. Bring to the boil, then take the pan off the heat and beat in the flour with a wooden spoon. Return the pan to the heat and stir vigorously to cook out the excess moisture. This will take a couple of minutes and the paste should start to come away from the sides of the pan.

Transfer the paste to a bowl and beat in the eggs one at a time until the mixture is smooth. Using a piping bag, pipe blobs of the mixture on to a non-stick baking mat: 2–3cm for snacks or starters, or 5–6cm to serve with filling and sauce as a meal with salad.

Sprinkle some grated cheese on top, then bake at 240°C/Fan 220°C/Gas 9 for 10 minutes. Reduce the heat to 200°C/Fan 180°C/Gas 6, open the oven door for a few seconds to let out excess steam, then bake for another 15 minutes.

Leave the gougères on a wire rack to cool slightly. If using the filling, mix the ingredients together. Make a hole in each gougère, then spoon in some filling or pipe it in with a piping bag.

If using the mornay sauce (see page 290), pipe it into the gougères and serve them warm. If you want to prepare the gougères in advance you can warm them through in a low oven before filling and serving.

PAIN À L'AIL

Garlic Bread

Try this different way of preparing a French favourite. Lightly grilled and drizzled with olive oil, my garlic bread is a perfect accompaniment to any soup or salad.

Makes 1 loaf

25G FRESH YEAST OR 12G DRIED

400ML LUKEWARM WATER

500G WHITE BREAD FLOUR

200G RYE FLOUR

1 TBSP OLIVE OIL, PLUS EXTRA
FOR BRUSHING

1 TBSP PICKED THYME LEAVES

2½ TSP SALT

Garlic Confit

12 GARLIC CLOVES, PEELED

2 TBSP OLIVE OIL

SALT

First prepare the garlic confit. Preheat the oven to 190°C/Fan 170°C/Gas 5. Bring a pan of salted water to the boil, add the garlic and cook for 30 seconds, then drain. Put the garlic cloves on a piece of foil, sprinkle them with the olive oil and a little salt. Wrap the garlic up loosely by bringing the corners of the foil together. Place the parcel in an ovenproof dish and cook in the oven for 1 hour. Leave to cool.

For the bread, dissolve the yeast in the water in a large bowl. Add the white and rye flours, oil, thyme and salt, mix well and knead for 5 minutes. Cover and leave the dough to rise in a warm place until doubled in volume.

Knock the dough back and knead it again for 5 minutes. Roll the dough out into a long flat oval shape and dot the garlic over it evenly. Fold the dough over on itself, then shape it into a loaf. Brush with a little olive oil, cover and leave to rise. Preheat the oven to 220°C/Fan 200°C/ Gas 7.

When you're ready to cook the loaf, make 3 or 4 cuts about 1cm deep across it. Cook the bread in the oven for 20 minutes, then turn the heat down to 200°C/Fan 180°C/Gas 6 and bake for a further 20 minutes. Cool on a wire rack before using.

PAIN À LA FARINE DE CHÂTAIGNES

Chestnut Flour Bread

Chestnut flour adds a lovely sweetness to bread and this loaf is perfect toasted for breakfast or to serve with salty charcuterie. You will find this style of bread in the Cévennes, parts of Provence and in Corsica, where chestnuts are grown in abundance. Chestnut flour on its own can be a bit heavy so I add some wheat flour to help. I like to use wholegrain spelt.

Makes 1 loaf

25G FRESH YEAST OR 12G DRIED YEAST

UP TO 400ML LUKEWARM WATER

350G SPELT FLOUR, PLUS EXTRA FOR DUSTING

200G CHESTNUT FLOUR

3 TSP SALT

Put the yeast in a large bowl and add 350ml of the lukewarm water. Stir to dissolve, then add both flours and the salt. Knead for 10 minutes until the dough is elastic and not sticky – you may have to add a little more water depending on the quality of the flour. Cover the bowl and leave the dough to rise in a warm place for 1 hour.

Knock the dough back and shape it into a round ball or your desired shape. Place it on a baking tray, dust with flour, then cover it with a cloth and leave to rise again for 30 minutes. Preheat the oven to 240°C/Fan 220°C/ Gas 9.

Using a sharp, thin-bladed knife, make 2 or 3 cuts about 1cm deep in the dough. Put the bread into the oven, then throw about a quarter of a cup of water into the bottom of the oven to create some steam. This helps to give the bread a good crust.

Bake the bread for about 35 minutes, then leave it on a wire rack to cool before slicing.

INFUSIONS ET LIBATIONS

Drinks

This chapter is about flavouring wines and spirits with fruit and herbs to make delicious liqueurs. These are easy to prepare, keep for ages and make wonderful presents. Some are alleged to have health benefits and improve the digestion! I've also included a delightful infusion to have at the end of a meal or before bedtime to help you relax and unwind.

VIN D'ORANGE
Orange—Flavoured Wine

Make this in January in the Seville orange season and come the summer you'll thank yourself. Serve this deliciously fragrant drink on the rocks as an aperitif or use it as a base for cocktails instead of vermouth. It's best to use Seville oranges, as their bitterness is just right for this drink, but if you can't get them I suggest you double up on the lemons. It's worth making quite a large quantity, as a bottle of this makes a lovely gift.

Makes about 3.5 litres

3 X 75CL BOTTLES OF DRY WHITE WINE

750ML CLEAR EAU DE VIE OR VODKA

360G CASTER SUGAR

6 SEVILLE ORANGES

1 SWEET ORANGE

2 LEMONS

4 FRESH BAY LEAVES

Pour the wine and eau de vie or vodka into a large non-reactive container – a plastic brewing kit bucket is ideal. Add the sugar and stir until it dissolves.

Wash the fruit well, then cut it up into small bite-sized pieces, collecting any juice that runs.

Add the fruit and bay leaves to the bucket and mix well. Cover tightly and leave to macerate for at least 90 days, stirring every now and then.

Pass the mixture though a fine sieve, pressing gently, then line the sieve with cheesecloth or muslin and pass it through again. Pour into sterilised bottles, seal and store for at least another month before drinking.

CRÈME DE CASSIS
Blackcurrant Liqueur

Use this liqueur for making a classic Kir (with white wine) or Kir royale (with champagne), or serve it over ice as an aperitif. It can also be made with blackberries or a mix of blackberries and blackcurrants.

Makes about 1.5 litres

500G BLACKCURRANTS

500G CASTER SUGAR

1 BOTTLE OF FULL-BODIED RED WINE (SYRAH OR MALBEC)

300ML EAU DE VIE OR VODKA

Wash the fruit, put it in a pan and crush it with a potato masher. Add the sugar and the red wine. Bring to a simmer, skim the surface, then pour everything into a bowl. Cover and leave to macerate in the fridge for 36 hours.

Pass the mixture though a very fine sieve into a clean bowl, add the eau de vie or vodka, then decant into sterilised wine bottles or old-fashioned lemonade bottles with stoppers.

Seal and leave for a couple of months before using. (See picture on page 268.)

CERISES À L'EAU DE VIE (GRIOTTINES)

Cherries in Alcohol

In France you can buy clear fruit alcohol for macerating fruit, but this works just as well with brandy or with vodka, which is what I've used here. Any variety of cherry is fine, but adjust the sugar if you have a really sour variety. I like to use the cherries as a garnish for cocktails or to give a kick to fruit salads or a bowl of ice cream — and the liqueur can be served over ice or as part of a champagne cocktail.

Makes 3 x 500ml jars

500G CHERRIES

200G CASTER SUGAR

750ML GOOD-QUALITY VODKA

250ML PORT

2 CINNAMON STICKS

Wash the cherries and remove any damaged or bruised ones. Mix the sugar with the vodka and port.

Place the cherries in sterilised, sealable jars and add the cinnamon sticks. Pour in the liquid and shake the jars a little to settle the cherries. They must be completely covered by the liquid — top up with a little more vodka if necessary.

Place in a cool dark place for at least 4 months and give the jars a shake from time to time.

INFUSION DE GINGEMBRE ET CITRONNELLE

Ginger & Lemongrass Infusion

I first tasted this in Mauritius and it's also popular in the Seychelles. It aids the digestion so is a lovely way to round off a rich or spicy meal. It's also good served cold and it's a great detox drink.

Serves 1

1 STICK OF LEMONGRASS

2 THICK SLICES OF FRESH ROOT GINGER

250ML JUST-BOILED WATER

1 TBSP HONEY (OPTIONAL)

Bash the lemongrass with the back of a knife to bruise it and release its aroma. Put it in a pot or jug with the ginger. Pour on the boiling water and leave to steep for 10 minutes. Stir in the honey, if using.

LE GÉNÉPI
Wormwood Liqueur

Wormwood is a mountain plant that grows at between 2000 and 3000 metres and it's the main flavour component in this liqueur. Served as an aperitif or digestif, it has many virtues – it stimulates the appetite, acts as a tonic for the digestion, prevents intestinal parasites and is used in the treatment of altitude sickness. A splosh in a cup of hot chocolate is delicious too!

Makes about 1.2 litres

1 LITRE VODKA

200G CASTER SUGAR

1 TBSP DRIED GÉNÉPI (WORMWOOD)

10 DRIED CAMOMILE FLOWERS

Place all the ingredients in a large sealable jar and mix well to dissolve the sugar.

Leave it to steep for 40 days, shaking the jar several times during this period.

Pass the liquid through a sieve lined with muslin into a large jug, then pour it into sterilised bottles.

PASTIS

Aniseed Liqueur

Served all over France, this is the go-to drink to serve as an aperitif or to sip while playing pétanque. Add a little mint syrup and it's called a 'perroquet'; with grenadine it's a 'tomate'. The main flavour is anise, but the different brands all have their own secret recipes. The thing they have in common is that they go cloudy when mixed with water. The home-made version doesn't cloud as much but is easy to make and even easier to drink!

Makes 1 litre

2 LIQUORICE STICKS

12 STAR ANISE

½ TSP FENNEL SEEDS

½ TSP CORIANDER SEEDS

½ TSP GREEN ANISEED

700ML GOOD-QUALITY VODKA

100G CASTER SUGAR

Chop the liquorice sticks and place them and all the spices in a dry pan. Warm them through over a medium heat to release the aroma, but do not toast them.

Remove the spices from the pan and grind them to a fine powder in a spice grinder or with a pestle and mortar.

Pour the vodka into a couple of sterilised, sealable glass jars, add the spice and liquorice powder and shake well. Leave the jars in a cool dark place for a week, giving them a good shake daily.

Put the sugar in a pan with 80ml of water and boil for 2 minutes, then set it aside to cool. Pass the vodka through a sieve lined with a muslin cloth, then add the sugar syrup. Leave to cool, then pour into sterilised bottles – wine bottles or lemonade bottles with screw caps are fine.

Seal and leave for a week before drinking.

VIN DE NOIX
Walnut Liqueur

There are many recipes for this delicious drink but this is one of the easiest. Served on ice as an aperitif or as an after-dinner drink, vin de noix is said to be good for the digestion and for cleansing the system! The walnuts must be green and unripe, picked before 24th June, the feast day of St John the Baptist.

Makes about 2.5 litres

10 GREEN WALNUTS

3 WALNUT LEAVES (OPTIONAL)

½ ORANGE, SLICED

325ML VODKA OR BRANDY (MINIMUM 40% ALCOHOL)

300G SUGAR

2 CLOVES

3 X 75CL BOTTLES OF WINE – ROSÉ, RED OR A MIXTURE (13–14% ALCOHOL)

Wash the walnuts and the leaves. Cut or break them into small pieces – wear an apron and watch out for the walnut juice, as it stains. Place the walnuts in a clean demijohn or a plastic brewing bucket.

Add the sliced orange and all the other ingredients. Mix well, cover and leave in a cool dark place for at least 100 days. Stir every week or so.

Filter the liquid through a sieve lined with muslin and then pour into sterilised bottles. Seal and leave to settle. Traditionally this liqueur is not served until Christmas.

SAUCES ET BASES

Sauces & Basics

You can, of course, buy stocks and there are some good ones available now, but it is always worth making your own when you have time — that way you know exactly what's in them. In this chapter I've also included some basic sauces and other recipes with a few tweaks to make them lighter or quicker than the traditional versions.

BOUILLON DE LÉGUMES

Vegetable Stock

This simple vegetable stock is ideal for soups and for cooking grains, such as buckwheat and Camargue red rice (see page 124).

Makes 2 litres

1 CARROT, PEELED AND ROUGHLY CHOPPED

2 SHALLOTS, PEELED AND ROUGHLY CHOPPED

1 SMALL ONION, PEELED AND ROUGHLY CHOPPED

2 CELERY STICKS, ROUGHLY CHOPPED

1 LEEK (GREEN TOP PART ONLY), ROUGHLY CHOPPED

1 BAY LEAF

A FEW THYME SPRIGS

6 PARSLEY STALKS

Put all the vegetables in a large saucepan and cover them with 2.5 litres of cold water. Add the herbs and bring the water to the boil.

Simmer for about 35 minutes, then strain the stock through a sieve before using. The stock can be kept in the fridge for up to 5 days.

BOUILLON DE POISSON
Fish Stock

Most fishmongers will give you fish bones and heads for stock if you ask. White fish, such as sole, whiting and turbot, are best. A good fish stock doesn't take long to make and it does make such a difference to your dish.

Makes about 2 litres

1KG WHITE FISH BONES AND HEADS

4 TBSP UNSALTED BUTTER

1 SMALL ONION, PEELED AND ROUGHLY CHOPPED

1 CELERY STICK, ROUGHLY CHOPPED

60ML DRY WHITE WINE

6 PARSLEY STALKS

1 BAY LEAF

Remove any gills from the fish heads, then soak the heads and bones in cold water for 3–4 hours. Remove them from the water and chop roughly.

Melt the butter in a deep pan and sweat the onion and celery over a low heat until softened. Add the fish bones and heads and cook for 2–3 minutes, stirring frequently.

Pour in the wine, turn up the heat and reduce by half. Add 2 litres of water and the herbs, then bring to the boil, skimming frequently. Lower the heat and simmer, uncovered, for 25 minutes.

Strain the mixture through a muslin-lined sieve and leave to cool. The stock can be kept in the fridge for 2–3 days or it can be frozen.

BOUILLON DE VOLAILLE

Chicken Stock

This is a simple white chicken stock, made without roasting the bones, for use in soups and light chicken and fish dishes. Ask your butcher to split the calf's foot for you.

Makes about 4 litres

2KG CHICKEN BONES OR WING TIPS

1 CALF'S FOOT, SPLIT

1 ONION, PEELED AND ROUGHLY CHOPPED

1 SMALL LEEK, ROUGHLY CHOPPED

2 CELERY STICKS, ROUGHLY CHOPPED

2 THYME SPRIGS

6 PARSLEY STALKS

Place the bones, or wing tips, and the calf's foot in a large saucepan, cover with 5 litres of water and bring the water to the boil. Skim off the scum and any fat that comes to the surface. Turn the heat down, add the remaining ingredients and simmer for 1½ hours, skimming occasionally.

Pass the stock through a fine sieve and leave it to cool. It can be kept in the fridge for up to 5 days, or you can freeze the stock until needed.

BOUILLON DE VOLAILLE BRUN

Brown Chicken Stock

For a brown chicken stock, the chicken bones are roasted before boiling which gives extra colour and depth of flavour.

Makes about 5 litres

2KG CHICKEN BONES OR WING TIPS

1 CALF'S FOOT, SPLIT

OLIVE OIL

1 ONION, PEELED AND ROUGHLY CHOPPED

1 CARROT, PEELED AND ROUGHLY CHOPPED

1 CELERY STICK, ROUGHLY CHOPPED

5 GARLIC CLOVES, PEELED AND ROUGHLY CHOPPED

1 TBSP TOMATO PASTE

2 THYME SPRIGS

Preheat the oven to 220°C/Fan 200°C/Gas 7. Put the bones, or wing tips, and the calf's foot in a roasting tin, drizzle them with olive oil and roast until brown.

Transfer the bones to a deep saucepan, cover with 5 litres of cold water and bring to a gentle simmer.

Meanwhile, place the roasting tin on the hob, add the vegetables and garlic and fry them until golden. Add the tomato paste, thyme and another litre of water. Bring to the boil, stirring well to scrape up any caramelised bits sticking to the bottom of the pan. Once the water is boiling, pour the contents of the tin into the saucepan with the bones and continue to simmer for 2 hours, skimming when necessary.

Pass the stock through a fine sieve and chill. It can be kept in the fridge for 5 days or it can be frozen.

BOUILLON DE VEAU
Veal Stock

Ask your butcher to chop the bones and split the calf's foot for you. This stock is ideal for the chicken breasts with Burgundy recipe on page 198.

Makes about 3.5 litres

1.5KG VEAL KNUCKLE BONES, CHOPPED

1 CALF'S FOOT, SPLIT

OLIVE OIL

1 LARGE ONION, PEELED AND ROUGHLY CHOPPED

2 LARGE CARROTS, PEELED AND ROUGHLY CHOPPED

1 CELERY STICK, ROUGHLY CHOPPED

2 GARLIC CLOVES, PEELED

2 THYME SPRIGS

½ TBSP TOMATO PURÉE

Preheat the oven to 220°C/Fan 200°C/Gas 7. Put the bones and calf's foot in a roasting tin with a little oil and roast in the oven, turning them occasionally until they're brown all over. Transfer them to a large saucepan.

Put the onion, carrots and celery into the roasting tin and roast them in the oven until golden, turning them from time to time with a wooden spatula. Pour off any excess fat and put the vegetables into the pan with the bones. Place the roasting tin over a high heat and add 500ml of water. Bring to the boil, scraping the bottom of the tin to loosen any caramelised bits, then pour everything into the pan with the bones.

Add the remaining ingredients and another 4½ litres of water and bring to the boil. Skim off any scum and fat, then turn down the heat and simmer gently for 3½ hours, skimming occasionally. Pass the stock through a fine sieve and leave to cool. The stock can be kept in the fridge for up to 7 days, or it can be frozen.

BOUILLON DE BOEUF
Beef Stock

Marrowbones, knuckles, ribs or oxtail tips with little or no meat on them are all fine for this stock. Ask your butcher to chop the bones up for you.

Makes about 4 litres

2KG BEEF BONES, CHOPPED

2 CARROTS, PEELED AND ROUGHLY CHOPPED

1 ONION, PEELED AND ROUGHLY CHOPPED

1 LEEK, ROUGHLY CHOPPED

2 CELERY STICKS, ROUGHLY CHOPPED

4 GARLIC CLOVES, PEELED AND CHOPPED

2 BAY LEAVES

OLIVE OIL

500ML WHITE WINE

1 TBSP BLACK PEPPERCORNS

Preheat the oven to 220°C/Fan 200°C/Gas 7. Put the bones in a large roasting tin. Add the vegetables, garlic and bay leaves to the bones and drizzle them with a little olive oil. Roast for about 30 minutes until the bones and vegetables are browned and caramelised, turning them a couple of times.

Transfer everything to a deep stock pan or a large saucepan, discarding any fat in the roasting tin. Put the tin on the hob and add the wine. Deglaze, scraping up any sticky bits from the bottom of the tin, then add this to the bones in the pan.

Add cold water to cover the bones and vegetables by at least 20cm. Bring to the boil and add the peppercorns, then turn the heat down to a very gentle simmer. Skim well and cook for at least 6 hours. You may need to top up the liquid with a little hot water from time to time to ensure the bones stay covered.

Leave to cool, then skim off any fat and strain the stock though a fine sieve. Use immediately or chill for later use. This stock freezes well.

PISTOU

Basil Sauce

This wonderfully fragrant sauce is similar to Ligurian pesto but without any cheese or pine nuts. It's usually used to flavour soups and salads but also makes a nice dip to serve with crudités. I know it's harder work but it is best to make this with a pestle and mortar if you can. If you do use a food processor, don't blitz the sauce until smooth – leave a little texture.

Makes about 200ml

200G BASIL LEAVES

1 TBSP COARSE SEA SALT

4 GARLIC CLOVES, PEELED AND CRUSHED

1 TSP GROUND BLACK PEPPER OR CHILLI POWDER

ZEST OF 1 UNWAXED LEMON (OPTIONAL)

160ML EXTRA VIRGIN OLIVE OIL

Place the basil leaves, salt and garlic in a mortar and crush them until coarse. Stir in the pepper or chilli powder, lemon zest and olive oil.

If making this in a food processor, mix until combined but not too smooth.

Spoon the pistou into a bowl, cover and store in the fridge. This keeps well for about 2 weeks.

SAUCE HOLLANDAISE LÉGÈRE

Light Hollandaise Sauce

The traditional version of this sauce is laden with butter and can be too rich and heavy. Thankfully, there is a lighter way of making it and the sauce is still delicious. Serve with vegetables, such as asparagus. It's also lovely with fish.

Serves 6

1 FREE-RANGE EGG, PLUS AN EXTRA YOLK

2 TBSP OLIVE OIL

2 TBSP BUTTER

1 TBSP WHITE WINE VINEGAR

2 TBSP CRÈME FRAÎCHE

SALT AND WHITE PEPPER

Crack the whole egg into a pan and add the extra yolk. Add 100ml of water, then the oil and butter and season well with salt and white pepper.

Place the pan over a medium heat and whisk with a balloon whisk until the mixture is light and fluffy. It should be thick enough to hold in the whisk as you lift it.

Take the pan off the heat and whisk in the vinegar and crème fraîche.

SAUCE MORNAY
Mornay Sauce

Another classic French sauce, this is similar to Béchamel, but enriched with grated cheese.
It's good served with gougères (see page 258).

Makes about 300ml

1 TBSP BUTTER

2 TBSP FLOUR

250ML WHOLE MILK

60G COMTÉ, GRUYÈRE OR EVEN BLUE
CHEESE OR A DRY GOATS' CHEESE,
GRATED

½ TSP SALT

WHITE PEPPER

GRATING OF NUTMEG

Melt the butter in a small pan. Add the flour and cook for 5 minutes over a low heat, then slowly add the milk, mixing well to avoid lumps.

Bring back to the boil and cook for 2–3 minutes. Take the pan off the heat, then beat in the grated cheese. Season with salt, pepper and a grating of nutmeg.

ROUILLE
Garlic & Pepper Sauce

There are many different versions of this delicious sauce, but this is one that I particularly like. Rouille is mostly served with fish soup or bouillabaisse but it's also good on salads or spread on slices of grilled baguette.

Makes a big bowlful

PINCH OF SAFFRON

1 TBSP LEMON JUICE

2 GARLIC CLOVES, PEELED AND CRUSHED

2 ANCHOVY FILETS

1 RED PEPPER

1 FREE-RANGE EGG YOLK

200ML OLIVE OIL

PINCH OF CHILLI FLAKES, TO TASTE

SALT

Put the saffron in a small bowl with the lemon juice and leave for 10 minutes to soften.

Chop the garlic and rinse the anchovies.

Roast the pepper under a hot grill, turning it regularly until blackened all over. Place it in a bowl, cover with cling film and leave to cool. When cool, peel off the black skin, remove the stalk, core and seeds and roughly chop the flesh.

Place all the ingredients, except the oil, salt and chilli flakes, in a blender and blitz until smooth. Slowly add the oil until the mixture emulsifies. Scoop into a bowl and season with salt and chilli flakes to taste.

Cover and store in the fridge for up to 2 weeks.

SAUCE VIERGE

Tomato & Herb Sauce

This sauce is best made a few hours before serving or even a day ahead to allow time for the flavours to develop. It's a perfect accompaniment for white fish or grilled vegetables.

Serves 4-6

6 TOMATOES, PEELED AND SEEDED

2 GARLIC CLOVES, PEELED AND FINELY CHOPPED

1 TBSP CHOPPED TARRAGON

1 TBSP CHOPPED CHERVIL

JUICE AND ZEST OF 1 LARGE LEMON

200ML EXTRA VIRGIN OLIVE OIL

1 TSP CORIANDER SEEDS, CRUSHED

SALT AND FRESHLY GROUND BLACK PEPPER

Finely chop the tomatoes and put them in a bowl. Add all the other ingredients, mix well and season with salt and pepper.

This is best served at room temperature, not cold from the fridge.

PURÉE DE TOMATES À L'AIL

Tomato & Garlic Purée

This can be used for adding flavour to salads or sandwiches or even as a dip. It's best to use dried tomatoes that still have some moisture – sometimes called sun-blushed or semi-dried. If you have a jar of tomatoes in oil, the oil can be used instead of, or as some of, the oil in the recipe.

Makes a small bowlful

120G SUN-DRIED OR SUN-BLUSHED
TOMATOES

4 TBSP OLIVE OIL

4 GARLIC CLOVES, PEELED AND
CRUSHED

1 TSP CHILLI FLAKES

HANDFUL OF BASIL LEAVES

Place all the ingredients in a food processor with 2 tablespoons of water and blitz until emulsified, but not too smooth.

Scoop into a bowl and cover. This keeps in the fridge for up to 2 weeks.

PÂTE BRISÉE
Traditional Shortcrust Pastry

This recipe is for a classic shortcrust and ideal for dishes such as the leek and salmon quiche on page 150.

Makes about 300g

200G PLAIN FLOUR

100G BUTTER, SOFTENED, PLUS EXTRA FOR GREASING THE TART RING

1 FREE-RANGE EGG

½ TSP SALT

Pile the flour on your work surface and make a well in the middle. Put the softened butter, egg and salt in the well and using your fingertips work them together until creamy. Gradually work in the flour and finally add a tablespoon of cold water to bring it all together. Do not overwork the pastry.

Wrap the pastry in cling film and leave it in the fridge until needed.

PÂTE SUCRÉE LÉGÈRE
Light Sweet Pastry

A crumbly sweet pastry, this is made with half cream cheese, half butter to give it a lovely light texture. It's a little less rich than the usual recipe but still indulgent and with great depth of flavour.

Makes about 350g

1 FREE-RANGE EGG YOLK

60G ICING SUGAR

1 PINCH OF SALT

½ TSP VANILLA EXTRACT

60G CREAM CHEESE

60G BUTTER, SOFTENED

200G PLAIN FLOUR

Beat the egg yolk with the sugar, salt and vanilla in a bowl until pale. Add the cream cheese and butter, then work in the flour to form a dough. Add a little more flour if needed. Don't overwork the dough.

Wrap the dough in cling film and leave it in the fridge to rest for 30 minutes before using.

FEUILLETAGE RAPIDE
Quick Puff Pastry

Traditional puff pastry takes up to 6 hours to make and needs a lot of resting time, rolling and folding. This method is much quicker and produces pastry that is just as delicious and flaky.

Makes about 550g

250G COLD BUTTER

300G PLAIN FLOUR, PLUS EXTRA FOR DUSTING

1 TSP SALT

Cut the butter into large dice, add them to the flour and salt in a bowl and work the butter and flour together loosely with your fingertips. Don't overwork it – you must be able to see bits of butter.

Add 160ml of cold water and bring the dough together. Wrap the dough in cling film and leave it to rest in the fridge for 20 minutes.

Roll out the dough on a floured surface to make a rectangle of about 20 x 50cm. Fold the top third down to the centre and the bottom third up and over that. Give the dough a quarter turn and roll, then repeat the folds.

Leave the dough in the fridge for another 20 minutes, then it is ready to use.

INDEX

301

INDEX

First published in Great Britain in 2018 by Seven Dials
an imprint of The Orion Publishing Group Ltd
Carmelite House, 50 Victoria Embankment
London EC4Y 0DZ

An Hachette UK Company

1 3 5 7 9 10 8 6 4 2

A CIP catalogue record for this book is
available from the British Library.

ISBN 9781409169246
ISBN 9781409169253

Photographer: Cristian Barnett
Design and art direction: Miranda Harvey
Editor: Jinny Johnson
Food stylist: Millie Simpson
Food stylist's assistant: Gemma Stoddart
Props stylist: Polly Webb-Wilson
Proofreader: Elise See Tai
Indexer: Vicki Robinson

Printed and bound in Italy

www.orionbooks.co.uk

FSC
www.fsc.org

MIX
Paper from
responsible sources
FSC® C015829

ACKNOWLEDGEMENTS

Special thanks to Millie and Gemma for helping to prep the most delicious food on shoot days, to Chef Rachel at Le Gavroche for testing the recipes, Cristian for his enthusiasm behind the lens, and Edwina my PA for finding the gaps in my diary and somehow managing to read my scribbled notes! Also to Miranda for her expert eye, Polly for the delightful props, and Jinny for helping me put the recipes into words.

I'd also like to thank to everyone at Orion, particularly publisher Amanda Harris and creative director Lucie Stericker, for having faith in French food.

Last but not least, thank you to Lilly Mandarano (www.thesupersparrow.com) for lending us her beautiful ceramic dishes for the food shoots.